PAULINE OLIVEROS
Photograph by the News and Public Service of Stanford
University. Used by permission.

The music of pauline oliveros

by heidi von gunden

THE SCARECROW PRESS, INC.
metuchen, nj, & london   1983

Library of Congress Cataloging in Publication Data

Von Gunden, Heidi, 1940-
    The music of Pauline Oliveros.

    "Catalog of compositions": p.
    Discography: p.
    Bibliography: p.
    1. Oliveros, Pauline, 1932-   . Works.
2. Oliveros, Pauline, 1932-   --Bibliography.
I. Title.
ML410.05834V6 1983   780'.92'4   82-21443
ISBN 0-8108-1600-8

CONTENTS

FOREWORD

Pauline Oliveros is a disconcerting figure to a great
many people. She has an apparent simplicity.
In her art this takes the form of a seeming lack
of compositional technique, even lack of seriousness in some cases. But this persona masks a
highly individual blend of directness, unconven-
tionality, humor, and self-effacement. Her theater pieces depend at least as much upon their
performers as upon her. Her meditative pieces
aim directly to bring the audience into participation and to strip each experience of unnecessary
elements. Even her concert pieces provide few
traditional structural elements to draw out the
intellectual participation of the listener.

Oliveros deliberately frustrates the effort
of the intellect to dominate art. She is certainly
a strong intellect herself, with ample ability to
hold her own in disputation and plenty of analytical expertise. But she abjures all this in favor
of a carefully planned involvement of sense perception, a meditative focus of attention and awareness, and a freeing of affective states from artistic manipulation. Her art seeks neither to stir
up emotions nor to fascinate the mind. This
takes it definitely outside the traditional mold.
It is as little "expressive" of her emotions as
John Cage's music is of his, and almost as independent of choice and taste; but unlike Cage,
she focuses directly upon psychological states
and general participation. The abstract functioning of chance plays no part.

As a person Oliveros evinces a similar
deceptiveness. Direct and forthright to a marked
degree, she seems almost devoid of artistic sensitivity. Nothing could be farther from the truth.

[v]

She cultivates an unadorned manner and appearance to such an extent that one would not readily take her to be the extremely subtle and delicate artist that she is.   Her practicality strikes one immediately, and is not an illusion.   But there is as well a thoroughly unworldly concern with matters the average person might well term "mystical."   It is a Zen-like mysticism, however, rooted in the ordinary and seemingly without system.

Her courage is almost breathtaking.   Witness her public avowal of homosexuality and a subsequent refusal to use this to publicize her music.   Witness also her abandonment of a teaching career to live reclusively.   Even her involvement in karate bears out this trait.

Pauline Oliveros has refused even as a teacher to serve the mere passing on of traditions.   She has sought to awaken the creative individual in each student, and to remain unwaveringly true to her concept of what art is.   Her concern with religion is equally pervasive, uncompromising, and nontraditional.

She is a powerful force in contemporary art and an innovator of timely basic ranges in the purpose and practice of art.

Heidi Von Gunden, a former pupil of Oliveros, brings penetrating insight to bear on this important composer.   Von Gunden's approach is direct and insightful, as befits her subject.   This study is an important first step toward a wider and deeper understanding of one of our best artists.

[Ben Johnston]

PREFACE

Pauline Oliveros, an internationally known American composer, has been in the forefront of music since the late 1950s. She is four years younger than Karlheinz Stockhausen, and her career parallels his in many respects. They both have written traditionally notated music, graphic scores, improvisations, theater pieces, electronic music, and sonic meditations. Frequently Oliveros preceded Stockhausen with innovative ideas about music and composition.

Her philosophy of art is influenced by an array of sources related to her interest in listening and consciousness studies. Her recent music can reflect a quiet Zen Buddhist holistic approach to art, nature, and life or the dynamic disciplines of the martial arts. Underlying these elements is her belief in artistic freedom, which she considers to be an implicit tenet of feminism.

Oliveros is an enigma. She plays the accordion, studies karate, and likes outrageous music. Some of her music requires that performers sit out-of-doors and respond vocally to the sounds of automobiles and airplane noises. She has written a two-hour-long piece in which runners circumnavigate a circle while musicians sound exotic instruments, perform sonic meditations, and move with colored sheets while a nude couple stands within a black-and-white circular tent. Sometimes she writes musical portraits that can be performed only by one particular person, but she also composes for amateurs and nonmusicians. She promotes listening, requiring the performers and audience to listen intently. Rarely does she use a proscenium stage; she prefers large spaces,

[vii]

gymnasiums, and the outdoors, where performers can surround the audience.

Even more unconventional is the self-revealing quality of her music.   She uses imagery personal to her, such
psychograms as elephants, crows, Beethoven, parrots, the
death of her grandmother, the birth of a niece, mandalas,
and dreams.

Some critics consider this musical freedom so con-
troversial that they reject her work, and aestheticians find
it difficult to explain her art.   Yet she has won prizes and
been successful with performances, recordings, and publications of her compositions.

Oliveros frequently collaborates with other artists.
She has composed musical scores for Merce Cunningham's
dances, improvised for Al Huang's T'ai Chi sessions, and
involved the poets Margaret Porter and Jackson MacLow in
her work.

Academia has honored Oliveros, even though she has
only a bachelor of arts degree.   She served five years on
the composer/librettist panel for the National Endowment for
the Arts, was director of the Center for Music Experiment
in La Jolla, received a Guggenheim fellowship, has been a visiting professor at Stanford and York Universities, and has
published numerous articles in professional journals.

Professors may look askance at her research because
she studies dreams, psychology, telepathy, oriental philosophy, myths, rituals, and karate, but her work cannot be
dismissed because her reputation is too impressive.   She
has been so successful that she resigned as full professor
at the University of California at San Diego, deposited her
entire archive of sources, correspondence, and writings at
the university's library, and moved from her coastal home
in Leucadia to an A-frame cabin at Mount Tremper, New
York, so that she could devote all of her time to composition and performance.

For some, Oliveros is a champion of feminism, but
she has never been a token woman.   Her success came before and is independent of the women's movement.   For
many, she is simply a champion of freedom in the arts.
Although it is too early to assess fully her contribution to
American music, it is quite possible that she will rank with

Charles Ives, Harry Partch, and John Cage as experimental-
ists who daringly rejected European concert tradition in order
to develop their own creativity.

Oliveros's catalog is so extensive and varied that it
is impossible to discuss all of her music in a book of this
size. Instead, I have selected what I consider to be her
most important works and have analyzed them with the intention of showing the reader how to listen to these unusual
compositions.

I wish to thank Electa Clark, Deane Ellen Clements, and
Ben Johnston for reading the manuscript and for their en-
couragement. I am grateful to the Research Board of the
University of Illinois for several grants that allowed me to
travel to the University of California at San Diego and to
Mount Tremper, New York. Lastly I thank Pauline Oliveros
for reading the manuscript and for providing generous answers to my many questions.

THE
MUSIC
OF
PAULINE
OLIVEROS

1: BEGINNINGS

Pauline Oliveros was born in Houston, Texas, on May 30, 1932. Although her birthplace and Hispanic surname are not significant in the development of her career, the Texan trait of rugged individuality is a prominent characteristic of her life and music.

As is generally the case with successful women visual artists, Oliveros inherited her artistic aptitudes. [1] Her maternal grandfather, John M. Gribbin, collected stringed instruments, and Pauline V. Gribbin, her grandmother, gave piano lessons until she was eighty years old. They had an only child, Edith Inez, who showed a talent for music and like her mother became a piano teacher. In 1929 she married John B. Oliveros Jr.; they had two children, Pauline and John. The family, including the grandparents, enjoyed playing cards and listening to the radio. Oliveros frequently reminisces about liking to tune her grandfather's wireless radio so that she could hear static sounds. She identifies this interest as the beginnings of her work with electronic music. [2]

In 1941 Oliveros's father deserted the family and joined the Air Corps, leaving Edith with the financial burden of supporting her two children. She gave piano lessons, accompanied dance classes, and raised chickens. Her mother, Pauline, helped Edith with the children, and the young Pauline formed close emotional ties to her grandmother, who died in 1973 at the age of ninety-four. Several years later Oliveros composed The Pathways of the Grandmothers (1976) for accordion and voice as a memorial. Oliveros gave a special performance of the piece on November 30, 1977, which

[3]

would have been her grandmother's ninety-eighth birthday,
and had a card picturing the two Paulines printed for this
occasion.   (The printing on the back of the card is in the
shape of a mandala, a form that Oliveros has used since
the 1970s.)

Although financial circumstances were difficult, Edith
Oliveros managed to provide music lessons for her children.
She started young John studying the accordion, an instrument
that fascinated his sister, and taught Pauline how to play the
piano.   Oliveros confesses that she was not too serious about
piano lessons, but was very enthusiastic when in 1945 she
was allowed to study accordion with Willard Palmer, a teacher she admires.   Her accordion study included transcriptions
of Bach Inventions and other serious keyboard pieces.   Perhaps the most important lesson that Palmer taught his young
student was to listen to combination tones, the added sounds
that sometimes are heard when two or more tones are played
together.   This intrigued Oliveros, and combination tones
were later to be an important aspect of her work with electronic music.

In addition to the accordion Oliveros taught herself to
play the tuba so that she could join her junior high school
band.   Later, in high school, she studied the French horn
and became a proficient performer.

Oliveros did not consider a performance or teaching
career, but while still in high school she knew that she
wanted to become a composer.   She had already begun to
develop aural skills by writing down tunes she heard on records, and in 1948 she even made wire recordings of her own
playing.   Realizing that she could easily imagine sounds internally, she was eager to learn how to write them down.
Oliveros says that she never thought it strange that she
wanted to be a composer since both her grandmother and
mother were strong role models of women who made serious
music their livelihood.

Also, her musical talent was a financial incentive.
When she was seventeen years old, she played accordion in
a polka band.   The experience was more valuable than the
money she earned.   One night the band tried to play German
polkas in a Polish hall (this was in the 1940s) and the musicians were angrily asked to leave.   From that time on
Oliveros was conscious of how music affects people.

THE THE
PATHWAYS PATHWAYS
OF THE OF THE
GRANDMOTHERS **+●+** GRANDMOTHERS
+●+
GRANDMOTHERS **+●+** GRANDMOTHERS
OF THE OF THE
PATHWAYS PATHWAYS
THE THE

IN MEMORY OF

PAULINE V. GRIBBIN

NOVEMBER 30, 1879 · 1973, 31 DECEMBER

BY

PAULINE OLIVEROS
accordion and voice
NOVEMBER 30, 1977, 7PM, 424 F ST, S.D., CA.

Memorial card for Pauline Gribbin

  Listening has always been important to Oliveros, but she is also concerned about the visual and theatrical aspect of her pieces. This may stem from some acting she did, playing the role of Hattie in Howard Richardson's Dark of the Moon at the Houston Little Theater. The acting, however, was not as interesting as the short biographical note in the program, which stated that Oliveros formed and conducted two orchestras: "The Texas Squares" and a dance orchestra.

  In 1949 she enrolled in the University of Houston as an accordion major and took the traditional freshman and sophomore theory classes, and in her junior year she registered for her first composition class. The teacher, Paul Koepke, wanted his students to write using Mendelssohn's Songs Without Words (1830) as a model. This was a frustrating experience because Oliveros did not want to write like someone else. She has recalled, "I rebelled. I used every exercise to reach further toward what I heard. I would go home and struggle for the pitches I needed at the piano. Foremost in my mind, though, were the qualities or colors (timbre) of the pitches, or how instruments other than the piano would be mixed together to form my composi-

tions.   I would find the pitches I want [sic] and form a mental image of the instrumental mix, and little by little I
learned how to write what I was imagining."3

But Oliveros was also gaining experience in the University of Houston's experimental dance-band-arranging class
taught by Ed Gerlach.   The laboratory situation of performing student arrangements taught the young composer practical writing skills and gave her an opportunity to play her
French horn in varied ensembles.   She was the only female
in the band; the Houston Post featured several articles about
the class with pictures of Oliveros and her male colleagues.

During this year she composed four pieces: Ode to
a Morbid Marble for piano solo (1951, her first composition),
Undertone for violin and piano (1951), Song for Piano (1952),
and Song for Horn and Harp and Dance Band (1952).   In the
spring composition recital Edith Oliveros played her daugh-
ter's Undertone with violinist Henry Lavaty, and then the
Song for Horn and Harp and Dance Band was performed as
part of the Fine Arts Spring Festival.   Oliveros's composition was on a program of works by Gounod, Mozart, Menotti,
and Gershwin.   The Houston Post's review of the concert
was uncomplimentary: "Her [Oliveros's] composition is of
only limited interest, and suffered in comparison to some
of the other works played."4   The criticism did not stop
Oliveros from pursuing her career as a composer.   It was
quite an accomplishment and a thrilling experience to hear
two of her own compositions performed at the end of her
first year of composition study.   Ever since then she has
always written with the intention of hearing her music.   She
is not interested in abstract works, such as symphonies,
that have little or no chance of being performed.

Dissatisfied with the University of Houston, Oliveros
decided to go to San Francisco in search of a composition
teacher who would understand how she was hearing sounds.
She left home with $300 and an accordion.

Notes

1.   Linda Nochlin discusses artistic family heredity and environment as necessary prerequisites for successful women
artists.   See her article "Why Have There Been No Great
Women Artists?" in Thomas B. Hess and Elizabeth C.

Baker, editors, Art and Sexual Politics (New York: Collier/
Art News Series, 1973), pp. 1-43.

2.   Oliveros writes about her sonic childhood memories in
a discussion of Valentine (1968), her theater piece using
electronic music, in Elliott Schwartz, Electronic Music
(New York: Praeger, 1973), pp. 246-249.

3.   Oliveros writes candidly about herself.   She describes
her awakening compositional interest in "To Make a Universe
of Sound: Four Visions, " Paid My Dues: Journal of Women
and Music, II, 4 (1978), 8-9.

4.   Houston Post, May 21, 1952.

2: THE EARLY PIECES

Oliveros's success began with her move to San Francisco, her home for fourteen years. The city was a haven for artists, and even today street musicians, actors, mimes, poets, and painters contribute to its milieu.

KPFA, the listener-sponsored Pacifica radio station in Berkeley, was an important voice in the cultural and political life of the entire Bay area, and the station's owners and music directors befriended Oliveros, especially during her early years in San Francisco. (It was during this time that Stockhausen was working at the Cologne Radio Studio in Germany.) KPFA pioneered listener sponsorship and was the model of alternative community radio programming. [1]

Two of its music directors, Robert Erickson and Wilbur Ogdon, were to play prominent roles in her career. When Erickson was music director of KPFA, he invited Oliveros and some of her friends to use the studio to record and study their improvisations, and later, when Ogdon became the first chairman of the Music Department of the University of California at San Diego, Oliveros was offered a faculty position there.

The station was the area's main source for hearing new music, and the station's owner, Pacifica Broadcast, even sponsored composition contests. (Oliveros would win the 1961 competition.)

It was not until 1954, several years after coming to San Francisco, that Oliveros enrolled

in San Francisco State College to complete her bachelor's
degree. She had left Texas at the end of her junior year,
and in the meantime she worked at the Pacific Public Service Company, gave music lessons, and played accordion on
club dates. To fund her education she obtained a license
to test milk for the city of Berkeley, a job that consisted
mainly of washing dishes.

While at San Francisco State, Oliveros played the
French horn in the school's wind ensemble and also performed the Brahms Trio (1865) for horn, violin, and piano.
In 1957 she received the Mu Phi Alumnae Scholarship from
the college. Oliveros soon realized, however, that San
Francisco State did not answer her need for a composition
teacher.

Fortunately she met Robert Erickson, who was then
teaching at the San Francisco Conservatory of Music.
Erickson heard Oliveros's Song for Piano and Prelude and
Fugue for String Quartet (1953) at a composers' workshop
that had been organized at San Francisco State, and he expressed interest in her music. Oliveros realized that
Erickson was the teacher who would understand how she
heard sounds. She studied with him for six years (1954-60)
and attended his composition seminars at the Conservatory.

Other young composers, such as Terry Riley, Loren
Rush, Stuart Dempster, and Ramon Sender, also studied
with Erickson, who was an exceptional teacher. His influence and supportive criticism were important to their development. These students became Oliveros's friends, and
Erickson was later to become her colleague and neighbor in
Leucadia, California, beginning in 1967.

Erickson, a former student of Ernst Křenek, had
taught in Minnesota before coming to San Francisco in 1953.
He took a practical approach to composition, asking questions like: "What do you want me as listener to hear in
this piece?" or "How are you going to end it?" He insisted
that his students be realistic and consider who was going to
play their pieces. They were to compose with the intention
of having performances. Oliveros liked this approach.

At that time Erickson was writing a book about the
contrapuntal aspect of music. Today he is widely known as
a composer and scholar of timbral research. [2] He often
shared his research interest with the class and instilled a

sense of wonder and a desire for experimentation by stressing the parallels between musical and scientific research. Students were encouraged to follow their own natural compositional inclinations, and he told Oliveros to improvise her way through a piece so that she could pay attention to the sound she was hearing. Erickson suggested that students collaborate with each other and performers in discovering interesting compositional materials.

Oliveros progressed rapidly. By the time she completed her bachelor's degree in 1957 she had composed the following: Essay for Piano (1954), Trio for Clarinet, Horn and Bassoon (1956), Serenade for Viola and Bassoon (1956, her only experiment with twelve-tone writing), Three Songs for Soprano and Horn with texts by Carl Sandburg and Walt Whitman (1957), and Concert Piece for Accordion (1957). Many of these pieces were performed at the San Francisco State composers' workshop and attracted some public attention, but none of this music is published. As precursors of her professional work, however, these compositions exhibit a characteristic meticulousness. The manuscripts are dated and extremely legible, with detailed explanations where needed. Oliveros rarely revised scores: she knew exactly what she wanted. She was assured of hearing at least a reading of her music because she composed for instruments that were available to her, often writing for her colleagues in Erickson's seminar. Frequently she would play the horn or accordion parts herself, since she was an accomplished musician on both instruments.

After graduation Oliveros continued to study with Erickson, but she considers her Three Songs for Soprano and Piano (1957) her first professional work. It was at this time, the late 1950s, that John Cage astounded the public with his use of indeterminacy in music, and Edgard Varèse's Poème électronique (1958) was heard at the World's Fair in Brussels, a highly publicized example of electronic music. In later years Oliveros would be influenced by Cage and, like Varèse, would have works performed at world's fairs. Meanwhile she was developing her own approach to creativity. It is with the Three Songs that the listener can begin to hear two emerging traits: imagery and improvisation.

The poetic imagery of song form was especially appropriate for her at this time. Oliveros's first inclination for musical composition was inspired by a poem she read in high school. She has always been interested in language (her later works are notated in prose) and is an avid reader.

For the texts of her Three Songs she chose two poems by Robert Duncan, "An Interlude of Rare Beauty" and "Spider Song," and Charles Olson's "Song Number Six" from his Maximus Poems. Oliveros met Duncan and heard him read poetry. He introduced her to Olson's work. She felt a certain affinity for these writers, because they belonged to the San Francisco avant-garde and were sensitive to the musicality of poetry. Duncan, particularly, knew Anton Webern's music and liked Webern's motion and brevity.

Duncan's "interlude of rare beauty" was watching a swimming seal.

> An interlude   of rare beauty
>
> The seal in the depraved wave
> glides in the green of it.
> All his true statement
> made in his mere swimming.
>
> Thus   we reclaim
> all senseless motion from its waves
> of beauty.   Naming
> no more than our affection
> for naming. [3]

Oliveros did not rely on a precompositional plan but took the seal imagery as the basis for her music. She mentally imagined sounds and rhythms that the text suggested to her. Both Erickson and Oliveros considered this an intuitive approach, and Oliveros has described her method of writing as slowed-down improvisation. She depended upon her ability to imagine sounds easily and, when necessary, used the piano to help locate pitches. She heard the seal imagery as sevenths and thirds in a mildly dissonant but rhythmically active piano introduction (see Example 1) and interlude while a difficult atonal vocal line reflects the rise and fall of the swimming seal. The piano adds disjunct and unrelated lines in its own wavelike texture.

Duncan's text is indicative of Oliveros's future interest in oriental philosophy and meditative art. His poem resembles a haiku, with its sparse but emotionally powerful statement about the momentary realization of natural beauty.

<u>Example 1</u>. Beginning measures of "An Interlude of Rare Beauty" from the <u>Three Songs</u>. Copyright 1976 by Smith Publications. Used by permission.

The oriental influence is also evident in the way Duncan titled his poem, "An Interlude .   of Rare Beauty." Oliveros ignored the spacing and dot. At this time in her life she was not sensitive to the implied meaning of this visual imagery, but later a circled dot, ⊙ , would assume structural and symbolic meaning for all of her music. Also, Oliveros accidentally omitted the phrase "from its waves" when setting the text to music, an error that shows she was not as yet totally sensitive to the rhythm and meaning of the words. But, as in haiku tradition, she used the power of suggestion. Her music implies "sealness." The aware listener then completes the meaning of Duncan's contrast between seal nature and the human thinking process and Oliveros's sound and motions.

        There is one more significant characteristic about "An Interlude of Rare Beauty" that is unique to Oliveros's work as a contemporary artist. The environment in which she lives is frequently heard in her music. Anyone who has visited the coastline of northern California notices the colonies of seals that inhabit this area, particularly near the famous Cliff House restaurant and Seal Beach, which is south of San Francisco, where the seals sun themselves on the rocks. This sight must have impressed both Duncan and Oliveros. Later Oliveros used the sounds and sights of the San Diego Zoo to influence some of her compositions, such as <u>El Relicario de los Animales</u> (an improvisational piece for chamber ensemble and singer, 1979) and <u>Elephant Call</u> (a piece for solo trumpet, 1975).

Example 2.   Measures 1 to 4 of "Spider Song"

Example 3.   Measures 15 to 17 of "Spider Song" showing the
second repetition of the text

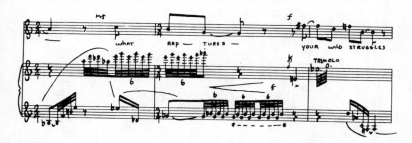

Example 4.   Measures 30 and 31 of "Spider Song" showing
the third repetition of the text.   Copyright 1976 by Smith
Publications.   Used by permission.

Oliveros's sonic imagery was even more apparent in Duncan's "Spider Song." He described the spider and its web as a blue bottle and a trembling veil. Oliveros repeated Duncan's short text three times using tremolo figures to represent the spider's struggles, trembles, and shakings. The intervals and lines are similar to those in the previous song; however, her more original idea was to separate the phrases of the poem gradually so that the piano part could create a musical web around and in between the text. Each musical statement of the text is new, yet changes in tempo and an agitated accelerando near the end provide unity. See Example 2 for the first setting of "what raptures your wild struggles" and Examples 3 and 4 for the second and third repetitions.

The third song of the set, "Song Number Six" from Olson's Maximus, is entirely different and seems out of place. Instead of using imagery Oliveros experimented with strict canonic writing. The song's short four-measure phrase is a canon between the three-voiced piano texture and the soprano line. There is no inherent relationship among the canonic process of the three motives (see Example 5), the shape of the lines, or the durations. Oliveros has never been comfortable with an abstract approach to composition, as in this canon. She sometimes designs processes that yield sonic results, such as tape-delay setups

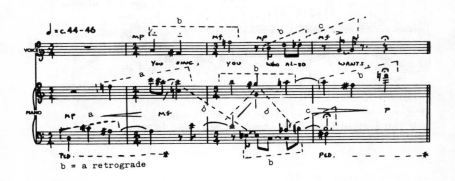

Example 5.   Canonic analysis of "Song Number Six." Copyright 1976 by Smith Publications. Used by permission.

or prescribed relationships among performers and sonic
materials, but other than this canon she has always written
music that has a personal meaning for her.

The Three Songs exhibit Oliveros's struggle to adapt
traditional materials to her own intuitive method of composition. She resisted the twelve-tone technique, which is sometimes a convenient organizational procedure for young composers since establishing a tone row lessens the number of
compositional decisions about pitch and harmonic action. She
felt that its tight organization was too restrictive and often
lacked emotional qualities. However, Oliveros used the
twelve-tone characteristics of featuring pointillistic lines
and fairly consistent interval patterning while avoiding obvious tonal centers, fifths, standard cadential patterns, and
octave doublings. She carefully chose her pitches so as to
eliminate close repetitions that might cause a hierarchy or
importance of a single pitch, as in tonal music. Yet the
order of presentation is not serial because it continually
changes. The overall impression is that this piece is at
least stylistically serial. Example 1 sounds like the exposition of a twelve-tone row until one reaches a repetition of
G before all twelve tones have been presented. (The G's
are circled in Example 1 and the two missing pitches that
would complete the row are E and B.)

Oliveros intended that eventually composing would be
her source of income, and by 1958 she was able to earn
some money writing incidental music for several plays and a
film documentary. She composed tonal melodies in the style
of Broadway show tunes with either piano score or lead
sheets. Sometimes Oliveros would provide accordion ac-
companiment for the performances. These were the skills
that she had learned in her dance-band-arranging class.

She even attempted several pedagogical works, and
planned to write Eighteen Accordion Pieces for Children
(1959), but completed only fifteen in pencil sketch. The
pieces are in the style of Béla Bartók's Mikrokosmos
(1926-39), with such titles as "Albert the Alligator," "Hy-
brid Folktune," "Camel Ride," "Dune Tune," and "Dragnet
Polka." It is regrettable that she did not complete this
project because it would have been a significant contribution
to the accordion's meager repertoire. She also composed
Horn Etudes (1959) intending to provide some challenging
contemporary studies for students. None of these works
has been published.

The accordion is a prominent symbol in Oliveros's career. She considers the instrument to be a victim of musical racism, as if the accordion were second class because it has been associated with ethnic music and relegated to playing transcriptions of popular classics. But she uses the accordion as her personal instrument and has composed solo accordion pieces for herself, the first titled Concert Piece for Accordion (1957). It is similar in style to the Three Songs, but is difficult to imagine how the music sounds because of the accordion's many timbral and registral changes, which Oliveros carefully indicated.

In addition to the Three Songs three significant works emerged from this early period: Variations for Sextet (1960), Trio for Flute, Piano and Page Turner (1961), and Sound Patterns for mixed chorus (1961). The years in which these pieces were composed, 1959-61, exhibit a rapid development of Oliveros's compositional style from her adaptation of the then-popular post-Webern atonal music to the abandonment of traditional notation, the adoption of graphic scores, and a free use of personal imagery and improvisation. These were the years that she won two important awards and several San Franciscan critics publicly supported her work.

If one compares the above pieces with her more recent meditations and ceremonies, it would seem that she has completely transformed her ideas about music and style, but several themes are apparent in all of her work. Imagery and improvisation are always present and listening is primary, but now her creativity begins to stretch the definition of music to include new ways of working with and thinking about sound and time.

Oliveros frequently uses some type of variation, not the traditional linear ornamentation, development, or transformation of a theme, but rather an Eastern concept of time as constant change, such as the philosophy of Taoism, the principle of the I Ching, or an acausal relationship that Carl Jung has called synchronicity. [4]

She studied these topics in the 1970s, but they are apparent in the way Oliveros wrote her compositions, listening to the materials and letting them suggest what should happen next. An absence of sequences, motives, and patterns tends to erase cause and effect, so that when listening to her music it is impossible to predict what the future action will be.

All of the above are noticeable in her Variations for Sextet of flute, clarinet, trumpet, horn, cello, and piano, composed between 1959 and 1960. This piece won the KPFA Pacifica Foundation Award, which helped to establish her reputation as a promising young composer. Like the Three Songs the opening measures of the Variations sound like the statement of a tone row. See Example 6. The sparse texture, interval patterning, groupings of usually two or three pitches per timbre, and the durational variety are somewhat similar to Anton Webern's Variations for Orchestra, Opus 30 (1940), and demand the same intense aural concentration.

Oliveros's Variations, however, are not organized serially, and the listener hears this because there are two repetitions on the first page that signal a free pitch selection. First, the pitch D is heard twice: as D^6 played by the flute in measure 1 and then as a cello D^2 in measure 2.[5] Second, a more prominent repetition of G^4-Bb^3 performed in succession by the clarinet in measures 4 and 5 creates a sense of tension because it delays the forward motion of the phrase. By the end of phrase 2, a measure later, the listener has begun to realize that the temporal aspect of the Variations will probably be more significant than pitch selection.

For awhile the piece progresses as one would expect with variations. There are obvious changes and contrasts. A legato variation is followed by a staccato one. Contrapuntal lines are replaced by homophonic groupings. It is even possible to trace a pitch theme visually for several pages in the score, although it is difficult to follow these pitches aurally because there are so many other changes occurring. Accelerandi and ritards abolish a constant tempo: sections are irregular in length, and numerous subdivisions and various durational lengths obscure the predictability of a rhythmic beat.

The listener needs some similarities and, finding none, begins to sense an emotional drama and tension. The composer is trying every kind of variety possible among the given materials. As the Variations progress the demands upon both the listeners' and performers' attention become unbearable until suddenly there is a dramatic change in measure 70. After a short pause a solo cello C^3 is extended for twenty seconds. The attack is almost silent. The tone begins nonvibrato and gradually becomes louder and develops a full vibrato. The appearance of this solitary

Example 6. Beginning measures of Variations. Copyright
1981 by Smith Publications. Used by permission.

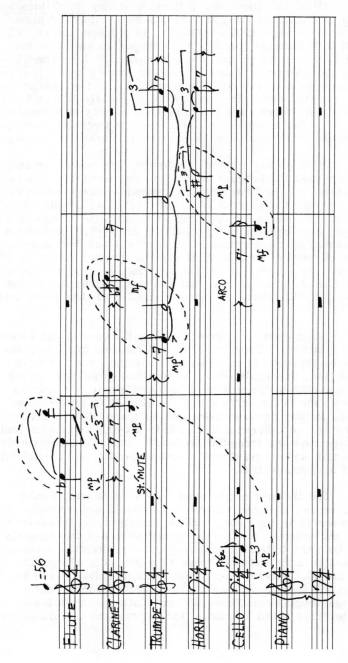

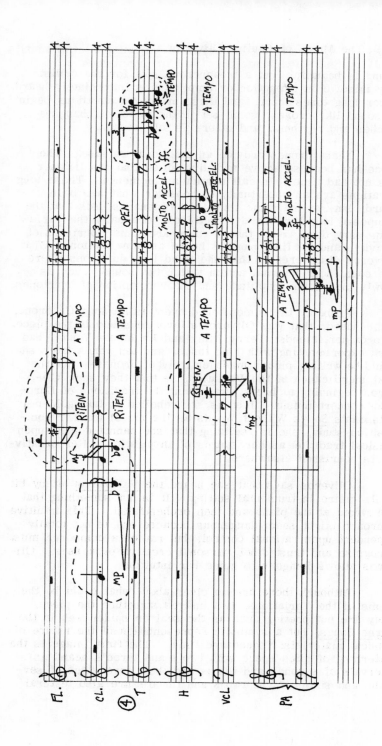

sound is beautiful, but a treacherous spot for the cellist. Any mistake in intonation or amplitude is immediately heard. Other long tones occur, and these prolonged durations begin to sound like drones, some set in the midst of changing pitches and rhythms, and others as solo sounds.

These drones provide an emotional release. The piece has been so active and diversified that the listener has not had time to recall particular moments. These long durations are an opportunity to consider what has been heard, but, at the same time, the listener senses that the composer has discovered something. Gradually the Variations slow down, even though there are some flourishes of activity, and the final page is heard as slow motion. What Oliveros discovered is that she liked long durations where one could hear internal action within the sound, such as slowly increasing amplitude and the recognition of overtones.

Probably the remembered event is the long C^3 drone, and, indeed, that was Oliveros's favorite sound in the piece. Two of her friends, Terry Riley and La Monte Young, had been experimenting with long tones, and ten years later she would be writing pieces made entirely of drones. But the real significance of the Variations is that they show Oliveros beginning to break away from the traditions of European concert music. Just as she rebelled at taking Mendelssohn's Songs Without Words as the model for her composition study, she is realizing that she cannot depend upon musical tradition as her source of inspiration. Her creativity is nourished elsewhere.

Oliveros says that she heard the Variations bit by bit in its entire instrumental setting. It is not something that she wrote at the piano and then orchestrated. This intuitive approach might seem dangerous because one is not totally dependent upon rational control, but rather a composer must recognize and trust other personal creative processes. Oliveros allows imagery to guide her intuition.

Although there are no clues about what could be the theme of the Variations, two images structure the piece. They are not poetic, such as the seal or spider web in the Three Songs, but a symbolic representation of the nature of musical materials: sound and time. The first image is the patterning of pitch space with two's and three's heard as intervals of seconds and thirds and their inversions of sevenths and sixths. The two's and three's are also textural because the varied use of articulation and dynamics causes the ear to group gestures together by similarity of attack, duration, register, and intensity. This grouping usually consists of two and sometimes three simultaneous lines, although the score is not visually contrapuntal. Consult Example 6, where the circled notes indicate the aural grouping. Notice that frequently the timbres within the groups are different, and the successful acoustical mix, juxtaposition, and superimposition of these timbres, while still maintaining a two- and three-part texture, is amazing, if one remembers that Oliveros had relatively little experience with orchestration at this time. The groupings by two's and three's were probably a way that her creative process unconsciously controlled her sonic imagination in the selection among so many possibilities.

Just the opposite situation occurs, an attempt at rational conscious structuring, beginning with measure 59, where Oliveros used proportional tempi with ♩ 108 = 2/3 of ♩ 72, and ♩ 54 = 4/3 of ♩ 72. Although she mentions the proportional tempi in the score's preface, these changes are not heard as metric modulations because there is no common link between the two tempi: one does not hear triplets become duplets in the new tempo, but the musicians must feel these changes so that the new tempo will be accurate.

Another reason why the metric modulation is not heard, is that a second image, a speeding up and slowing down, is also an important part of the Variations. This causes a variety of durations almost equaling the number of color changes. Each gesture is a combination of short and long, and no two gestures are the same length, as can be observed in measures 1-3 of Example 6. Also, the shape of this first phrase (measures 1-3) is characteristic of the motion of the entire piece. Cadences are long durations followed by a shorter one, with pitch frequently rising a third (the F^4-A^4 in the trumpet line is an example). This creates a sense of forward motion, which is necessary when a piece consists of small fragmentary gestures.

Oliveros sometimes used tempi as if they were timbres, juxtaposing and superimposing several upon each other, thereby causing one to hear two or three different tempi simultaneously. The sense of motion and rhythmic complexity is interrupted by the drone, and, oddly enough, the first drone appears in the section featuring metric modulation. Actually the drone is the real modulation, where

the listener switches from trying to hear everything at once
to listening to the sound within a single sound.

Two San Francisco critics sensed the importance of
this Oliveros work, although their reviews did not discuss the
musical aspects of the piece.   Alexander Fried, the music
critic for the San Francisco Examiner, described his reaction to her Variations: "... her piece was alive and fascinating every moment.   It had atmosphere.   It had emotional
value and a continuing suspense and fulfillment."[6]   Alfred
Frankenstein, writing for the San Francisco Chronicle, had
a similar response: "The Oliveros is intensely serious,
forceful, vastly dramatic in its implications, and truly symphonic in its breadth of values."[7]

Her next important composition was Trio for Flute,
Piano and Page Turner (1961); however, Trio for Accordion,
Trumpet and String Bass is also listed in her catalogue as
being composed in 1961.   This is not an important work in
her output because the musical ideas are too confined, and
few musicians would consider the accordion a serious instrument.   All of the Trio's five short movements (actually
written between 1959 and 1961) have short gestures formed
by interval patterning of thirds and seconds, which are shared
and mixed among the three instruments.   Often the accordion
provides a sustained cluster that is punctuated by short attacks from the trumpet and string bass.   Differing subdivisions and contrasts among long and short durations abolish
a sense of periodicity, but the overall time sense is too re-
stricted.   The piece needs to be either shorter and more
intense, like the Webern Bagatelles for string quartet (1913),
or designed so that the ideas can expand in a freer amount
of time.

All of the flaws in this piece were corrected in Trio
for Flute, Piano and Page Turner, Oliveros's last piece in
traditional notation.   Although it is an elaboration of the
gestures and ideas displayed in the Variations, there is a
new quality of visual imagery that adds a theatrical aspect
to her work.   An essential member of the ensemble, the
page turner silently depresses certain piano keys to add
resonance to other sounds.   At one point he or she is required to depress the keys "expressivo!"   Visually the piece
is interesting to the audience because the page turner is obviously quite busy, and there is even one page that the pianist must turn for the page turner.   But Oliveros intended
that these actions be more than humorous.   The piece is a

real trio, and the depressed keys are necessary to create the resonance that she desires.

Oliveros experimented with the sounds of a prepared piano, an innovation that John Cage had popularized in the late 1930s, and her interest in timbre might suggest that she would want to feature these sounds in her Trio. Nevertheless, she was very conservative in the techniques she used. A low A^1 is prepared with a Pink Pearl eraser, and there are several pizzicati within the piano (and of course the page turner silently depresses keys), but the interesting aspect of the piece is the mix of flute and piano sounds. Sometimes it is almost impossible to distinguish between the two.

The Trio and Variations are similar, as is noticeable when comparing the opening phrases of each piece in Examples 6 and 7. The intervals, phrase shape, and rhythmic motion are the same. Both works are linear textures with frequent tempo changes, but the Trio's composed timbres are more extensive and successful. Dynamics, attack, and coordination between the two instruments are carefully controlled. Registral differences are used to their full advantage, as in measures 11-12 in Example 8, where a single line travels between the extremes of both instruments. Drones emerge, as in the Variations, but this time Oliveros experiments with microtonal tuning, which is one way to alter flute timbre and listen to the internal action within a sound.

Resonance is another experimental approach to timbre alteration. Depressed piano keys and the differences among the piano's three pedals add shimmering and dry qualities to the piano sound. An additional aspect of the damper pedal and the depressed keys is an echo effect, when the residue of previous sounds begins to accumulate. Musically this also happens when both instruments interact with each other's gestures. Later Oliveros would explore accumulation and interaction as the materials for her compositions of electronic music.

Like most of her work the piece is sectional, caused by asymmetrical phrases and segments of silence. And again it is not the shape but the moment-to-moment change and interaction among the performers that create the interest.

In comparing this piece with other works for flute and piano, such as Olivier Messiaen's Le Merle noir (1950) or

Example 7.   Opening measures of <u>Trio</u>.   Copyright 1977 by
Smith Publications.   Used by permission.

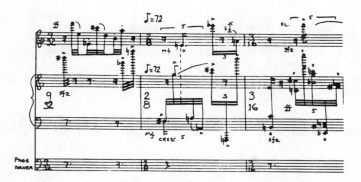

Example 8. Single line using the extremes of both instruments. Copyright 1977 by Smith Publications. Used by permission.

Aaron Copland's Duo (1971), one wonders why the Oliveros work has not been performed more often. Probably it is because the Trio is extremely difficult, more so than either Messiaen's or Copland's pieces. The coordination must be exact or the right timbres will not be created. Also, the piece was not published until 1977, although Oliveros had given copies to friends so that isolated performances have occurred in Iowa, New York, and Illinois. The Trio is available on "New Music for Woodwinds" (Advance Recording FGR-9S).

Morton Subotnick, a colleague of Oliveros at the San Francisco Tape Music Center, wrote about her Trio in Perspectives of New Music in 1963. [8] His analysis was the first serious analytical attention given to her music. Subotnick considered the piece to be variations of two motives initially stated in the first phrase as a slow flute gesture followed by a fast piano motive. See Example 7.

Subotnick's opening description of the Trio reflects the qualities that the San Francisco critics were recognizing in her work. He wrote: "Oliveros' Trio ... unfolds, without pretension, as a dramatic and unrestrained gesture through simple materials that are handled in such a manner that even the work's most complex events are clearly comprehensible. The flute and piano are treated with great care for their unique qualities...."[9]

Unfortunately, many readers find Subotnick's article ambiguous, as he unsuccessfully tries to analyze the piece tonally and formally. The listener does not follow tonal progression or even a formal plan, and this traditional approach does not explain the discoveries that Oliveros had made about the internal action within a sound or her use of imagery.

The Trio was the last of her strictly notated pitch pieces, and had Oliveros continued composing in its style, she probably would have reached a point of stagnation. Instead she turned to a new direction.

This change occurred with Sound Patterns for mixed chorus (1961). Sound Patterns is one of her better-known works, since it won the Gaudeamus Prize for the Best Foreign work in 1962 and is available on two recordings: "Extended Voices" (Odyssey 32 16 0156) and "20th Century Choral Music" (Ars Nova AN-1005). The medium she selected was an a cappella mixed chorus, and the text was phonetic sounds that she chose for their timbral possibilities. See Example 9.

The piece was innovative and unusual for the time, and many listeners of the recordings find it hard to believe that these a cappella sounds were strictly notated and performed without electronic manipulation. But Sound Patterns is an easy piece for listeners, although it is extremely difficult to perform. The composition is short (about four minutes), and the ideas are formally presented in a classic three-part design: an exposition (measures 1-12), where the vocabulary is stated; a development (measures 12-46), where the sounds are modulated and manipulated; and a recapitulation (measures 47-56), recalling initial material.

It was at this time that Oliveros began to work seriously with electronic music (the topic of Chapter 4), and Sound Patterns shows how her sonic imagination was influenced by the possibilities of this new medium. The actual sounds of the piece can be categorized into four types of sounds and techniques that are used in electronic music. They are: 1) white noise, 2) ring-modulated sounds, 3) percussive envelopes, and 4) filtered techniques. These sounds, labeled in Example 8, can be considered the main motives of the piece.

In electronic music white noise (the presence of all

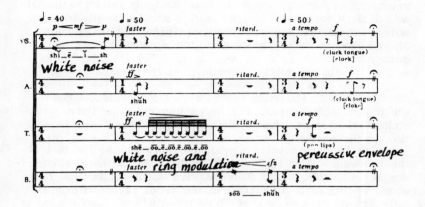

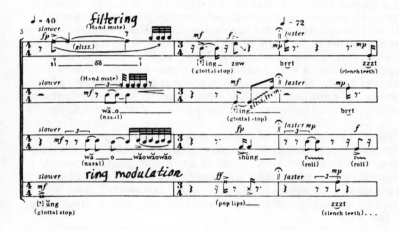

Example 9. First page of <u>Sound Patterns</u>. Copyright 1964 by Edition Tonos. Used by permission.

pitches sounding randomly) is frequently colored by selecting certain areas or band widths of noise to be heard.   This creates a variety of possible noiselike timbres.   The initial sound of Oliveros's piece is "sh," a vocal example of white noise that sonically permits a broad band of hissing sound. She colored this "sh" white noise by substituting various consonants, such as s, z, wh, p, t, h, ct, d, ch, th, k, and sw to change subtly the quality of the sound.

She was also able to imitate ring modulation (another electronic technique) vocally by rapidly changing the vowel content of certain sounds.   In electronic theory ring modulation is the result of two signals interacting with each other so as to produce a third signal, the only audible product of the process.   It is rather difficult to make a direct comparison between this studio technique and vocal production; however, changing the formation of the vocal cavity to produce different vowel sounds resembles the kinds of sounds used in ring modulation.   A classic example is singing the word "Hawaii" on the same pitch and carefully mouthing each vowel sound.   If one listens closely, distinct changes of timbre occur with each changing vowel.   See Example 9 for instances of ring-modulated sounds, and notice how Oliveros carefully notated the diacritical markings for each vowel so that the kinds of sounds she wants can be accurately produced.   A detailed legend of pronunciation symbols prefaces the score, so there is no doubt as to the desired timbre.

The third electroniclike motive is a series of percussive envelopes titled "lip pops," "tongue clicks," "snap fingers," and "flutter lips."   Although these sounds resemble childlike sonic play, they are used in a serious context and are difficult to perform because they demand a strict ensemble precision.   Examples can be seen on the first page of the score.

Filtering, or muting, is used in both electronic and acoustic music to reduce and change certain qualities of the original sound.   Oliveros designed several ways that singers could alter their vocal sound.   One was the use of the hand to mute the mouth (Example 9, measure 5); another was sounding the consonant "M" with tightly closed lips; and the third was singing through clenched teeth (Example 9, measure 7).

This is the basic material of the sonically interesting **Sound Patterns,** but even more fascinating is the craft and

technique used in shaping, mixing, and transforming. <u>Sound
Patterns</u> is Oliveros's most carefully composed piece. As
in her other works, there is continual variation; yet each
phrase presents a logical outgrowth of the preceding material
so that a sense of unity and variety is always present. For
example, phrase 1 uses four varieties of white noise:
shi-ē-i-sh, shuh, shē-o͞o-ē-o͞o-ē-o͞o-ē-o͞o (white noise combined with ring modulation), and s͞o͞o-shŭh followed by a
cadence of pop lips and two cluck tongues. As can be seen
and heard from the above example, no two utterances of
white noise are the same, but the listener is definitely
aware that a sonic gesture is being formed and soon will
be modulated.

The second phrase introduces muting while mixing
ring modulation with white noise (as in "shung" sung by the
tenors in measure 6), and the third phrase features percussive sound and new attacks. "Wht" becomes a version of
white noise; "bbbbbbbbt" (flutter lips) is a new percussive
sound, and "pow-wowōwowōwowo" is another ring modulation.
The separate dynamic markings for each sound and frequent
tempo fluctuations clearly define the phrase structure so that
the listener recognizes an initiation and conclusion of musical ideas.

As <u>Sound Patterns</u> progresses, one hears a reorgani-
zation of material. Rhythmic motives also help the listener
in following this development. Most ring-modulated sounds
are set in the context of minute subdivisions of the pulse
into six, seven, or eight thirty-second notes. A similar
kind of rhythmic motive is used with hand muting (see measure 5 of Example 9) and is also reflected in the flutter lips
of "bbbbbbbbt." Percussive sounds are short, but nonpercus-
sive sounds sometimes have percussive endings, which are
notated with a downward arrow indicating that the ending
consonant should be muffled or damped.

In contrast to these very short sounds, longer durations are heard beginning at measure 27. A contrapuntal
texture and later <u>divisi</u> parts help to create a sustaining
quality, and even a seven-layered texture for several measures. The thickest texture, however, is one improvised
measure that links the development to the recapitulation.
Oliveros carefully controls the improvisation, limiting timbre (only pop-lips or cluck-tongue sounds); the number of
attacks (five per person); and the sense of duration (each
beat has a different tempo).

The amount of restraint in this improvisation, the economy of form, and the obvious attention to how the listener will hear it are Sound Patterns's winning qualities--which certainly impressed the judges of the Gaudeamus Foundation.

In addition to its craft Sound Patterns was outrageously creative for its time and historically preceded similar vocal compositions by György Ligeti and Stockhausen. In fact Ligeti was one of the judges for the Gaudeamus competition, and he explored similar kinds of unusual vocal sounds in his pieces Aventures (1962) and Nouvelles Aventures (1962-65). Stockhausen composed Momente, his vocal linguistic piece for soprano, four choral groups, and thirteen instruments, between 1961 and 1962 on a commission from the West German Radio in Cologne. It is curious that he revised the work in 1965. The Dutch Radio Chorus performed Sound Patterns in 1962 and one can only speculate how much the Oliveros work influenced these two composers. Her piece was known to the European community: when Erhard Karkoschka assembled his book on Notation in New Music (the German edition was published in 1966 and the English version was available in 1972), he included a page from Sound Patterns as well as Stockhausen's Momente and both of Ligeti's Aventures as examples of the most recent work done in the area of vocal music. [10]

Although Edition Tonos Darmstadt published Sound Patterns in 1964, the score has been difficult to obtain in the United States. (It was available from Joseph Boonin Inc. but has now been assigned to European-American Distributors.) The rather long delay in publication was unfortunate for Oliveros. Many American audiences know the piece through performances by Kenneth Gaburo's New Choral Music Ensemble, active at the University of Illinois in the late 1960s, and by the Brandeis University Chamber Chorus, conducted by Alvin Lucier. Gaburo's ensemble even performed the piece at the world's fair at Montreal in 1968.

Notes

1.   The history of KPFA, along with KPFK in Los Angeles and WBAI in New York (all Pacifica-owned stations), is documented in Eleanor McKinney, editor, The Exacting Ear (New York: Pantheon, 1966). KPFA's current music director is the composer Charles Amirkhanian.

2.   See Robert Erickson, The Structure of Music: A Listener's Guide (New York: Noonday, 1955).   His more recent work is Sound Structure (Berkeley: University of California Press, 1975).

3.   Reprinted by permission of the poet.

4.   For an excellent discussion of synchronicity see Ira Progoff, Jung, Synchronicity, and Human Destiny (New York: Delta, 1973).

5.   The register numbering is standardized international acoustical terminology.   Middle C is C^4, and the numbers increase as the registers are higher.   Each successive C begins a new register.

6.   San Francisco Examiner, April 20, 1960.   The Variations for Sextet were performed at the 1981 Cabrillo Music Festival and reviewed by Richard Pontzious, San Francisco Examiner, August 21, 1981.   He found the piece difficult to understand and wrote that the music was "as cold as ice." Pontzious considered Oliveros's Sonic Meditations to be much more successful.

7.   San Francisco Chronicle, April 20, 1960.

8.   Morton Subotnick, "Pauline Oliveros, Trio," Perspectives of New Music, Fall-Winter 1963, pp. 77-82.

9.   Ibid., p. 77.

10.   Erhard Karkoschka, Notation in New Music (New York: Praeger, 1972), pp. 132, 156-161, and 122.

3: IMPROVISATION

In the 1950s composers began to experiment with ways of allowing more creativity for the performer. Notation became more flexible, often only specifying pitch ranges and suggesting freer rhythms, like "as fast as possible," or so many sounds within a given time period. The jazz tradition provided models of how groups of creative musicians could work together following a general outline of chord progressions and presenting what seemed to be spontaneous music.

Soon interested composers and performers began to form improvisation groups similar to the jazz ensembles. Some of these were associated with universities, such as Lukas Foss's Improvisation Chamber Ensemble at the University of California, Los Angeles, and Larry Austin's New Music Ensemble at the University of California, Davis. Often an improvisation group provided an opportunity for musicians and other artists to be independent of an institution. The ONCE group at Ann Arbor, Michigan, the Sonic Arts Group, and the San Francisco Tape Music Center were able to fund themselves through concerts, tours, and grants.

Some musicians and critics found it difficult to accept improvisation as a serious compositional mode. They wondered how anyone could sign his or her name as composer and whether the piece would be recognizable if performed again. But significant pieces like Foss's Time Cycles (1960) and Echoi (1963) were beginning to emerge as the result of a composer working with an improvisation group.

In 1957 Terry Riley, Loren Rush, and

[32]

Oliveros formed an improvisation group that met weekly and tape-recorded their sessions at KPFA. Since they wanted to play intuitively and without planned directions, the group found that the best procedure was to play, listen to the tape, and then talk about what they had done. These improvisations were practical lessons in ear-training. Oliveros discovered that she and her friends began to listen critically while performing, and because the tape confirmed what they had already heard these experiences developed their real-time listening skills.

Oliveros believes that her improvisation group predates Lukas Foss's Improvisation Chamber Ensemble, which was formed at the University of California at Los Angeles also in 1957. She recalls that sometime in 1957 Foss and his ensemble performed in San Francisco. Oliveros's group was disappointed in the Improvisation Chamber Ensemble's concert because the players used notated instructions and the sounds they produced were familiar and conservative. Later, when Oliveros and her friends spoke to Foss and described the work that they had been doing, he disapproved of their approach to free improvisation, saying that if the Improvisation Chamber Ensemble were to improvise in this way the result would be utter chaos.[1]

In 1961 she and some of her colleagues in Erickson's seminar formed another improvisation group called "Sonics." Encouraged by Erickson, Sonics established an electronic-music studio at the San Francisco Conservatory, and in eight weeks they presented a special concert featuring improvisation and electronic music. Later that year the group changed its identity and became the San Francisco Tape Music Center, which for some time was one of the leading new-music centers in the country.

Alfred Frankenstein, by now well aware of Oliveros's promising career, attended one of the concerts at the San Francisco Conservatory and wrote a favorable review about an improvisation using electronics. He reported the following:

> Tape recorder music was the latest thing until Saturday night, when it was capped by something newer still in a concert at the San Francisco Conservatory of Music.
>
> This thing that is newer still has no special name as yet. It was exemplified by an improvisa-

tion wherein two musicians, Pauline Oliveros and Morton Subotnick, worked with two others, Lynn Palmer and John Graham, who know how to act and speak and have a gift for saying things that are so outrageously inconsequential as to take on a strange kind of meaning.

> While musicians were busy, mostly with percussive sounds, and the two others were acting and singing and what not, Ramon Sender was taping the goings-on, and the taped sound came back, often in greatly altered forms, on speakers located at various points in the hall. As a result, the past of this improvisation became part of its present, and this use of the past as both substance and subject for an improvisation in the present seems to be a most remarkable idea.... I found it, even in its overextended form of Saturday night's program, one of the most stimulating things that has happened in years. 2

Oliveros was particularly interested in group improvisation because it made her listen carefully and stimulated her own creative ideas. She experimented with ways of controlling improvisation in her compositions. At first she allowed only a measure of freedom, as in Sound Patterns, while in her electronic music she designed the arrangement of the electronic equipment and then improvised the entire piece as a real-time performance. Improvisation, already her compositional method, also became her working method for research about acoustical timbres, electronic music, theatrical materials, ritual, ceremony, consciousness, and audience participation.

Many people have heard one of her early improvised pieces, Outline for Flute, Percussion, and String Bass (1963) on the recording "The Contemporary Contra Bass" (Nonesuch H-71237), featuring Bertram Turetzky performing pieces by John Cage, Ben Johnston, and Pauline Oliveros. There is some confusion about the title of Oliveros's piece. Media Press published it as Trio for Flute, Percussion, and String Bass, but its true title is Outline.

Although Oliveros considers her Outline to be an improvisation chart, the piece sounds extremely controlled, especially in the beginning, where definite pitch areas, mixed timbres, and strict but shifting tempi begin to emerge. See Example 10. One hears a unity that demands the careful listening and coordination expected in trio writing, but yet the piece is difficult to follow. The listener senses a conflict between freedom and control, not knowing how to reconcile the obvious compositional strictness with the concept of improvised spontaneity. Oliveros's idea was to limit the context of the improvisation to four possibilities: 1) pitch given but rhythms free, 2) everything strict except pitch, 3) free durations but suggested phrase structures, and 4) freed from all directions.

She intended that the composed sections, as in Example 10, would prepare and influence the improvised segments (see Example 11). As in many of Oliveros's early pieces, however, there are breaks in the emotional quality of the music. The listener does not know what to follow: the progress of the composition or the progress of the improvisation. One wonders: is the attentional problem the fault of the listener, composer, or performers?

Oliveros says that there was a performance error in the master tape. Nevertheless, the real problem is asking musicians to switch rapidly several times between being in a traditional performance mode realizing specific material and being in an improvisational mode relying upon spontaneous creativity. What becomes the true enjoyment of the piece is listening to Turetzky demonstrate new string techniques that were popular in the early 1960s. Fortunately, there are other recordings of Oliveros's improvised electronic music that are more successful. Later she solved the problem of how to generate dynamic improvisational material in such pieces as The Witness (1979) and El Relicario de los Animales (1980).

In the mid-1960s Oliveros began to experiment in an improvisational genre that I call "musical portraits." These works are commissioned, and they are so tailored to the personality and talents of the individual that only that person can perform them. Both visual and sonic images produce a musical photograph of the performer, and although these pieces are theatrical, they are included here as examples of how Oliveros used improvisation during this time.

Stuart Dempster, a trombonist and former classmate and improviser, commissioned Theater Piece for Trombone Player (1966). With the choreographer Elizabeth Harris, Oliveros created a mixed-media piece in which Dempster performs with garden hoses and moves about a complex stage design while accompanied by an improvised tape of

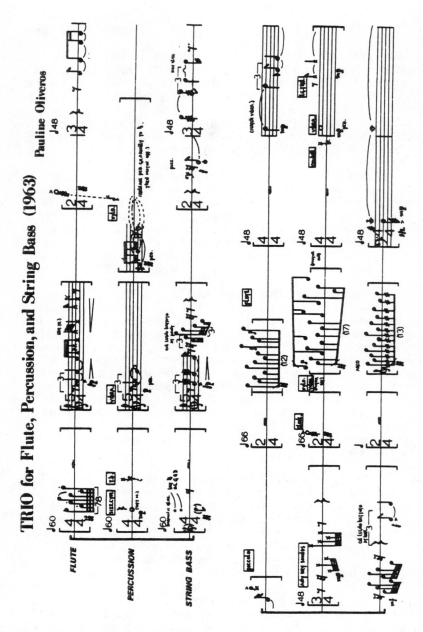

Example 10.   First page of Outline for Flute, Percussion, and String Bass.   Copyright © Media Press, Inc., 1971. All Rights Reserved.   Used by permission.

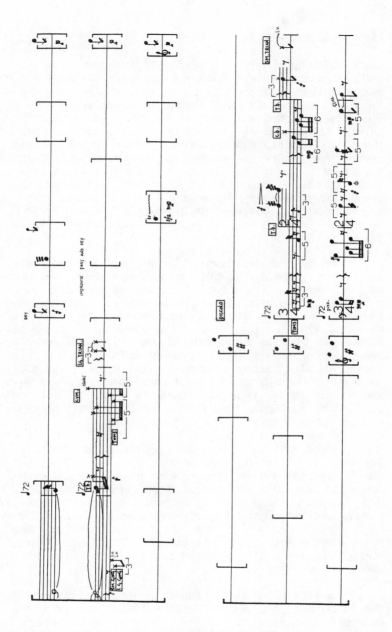

Example 11.   Improvised section from Outline for Flute,
Percussion, and String Bass.   Copyright © Media Press,
Inc., 1971.   All Rights Reserved.   Used by permission.

his astonishing trombone vocabulary.   Dempster practices
hatha yoga and is noted for his amazing breath control.   He
has studied circular breathing required for the didjeridu, a
log instrument used by the Australian aborigines.   Although
I have never heard and seen the piece, I can well imagine
Oliveros's collection of unusual trombone sounds coupled with
Harris's directions that the agile Dempster improvise with
garden hoses, blow out candles, and crawl about a stage as
a portrait of the person Stuart Dempster that is not revealed
in the traditional repertory for trombone.   Dempster has
played the piece many times on his concert tours, including
a performance in Carnegie Hall, which helped to establish
Oliveros's reputation as a composer of avant-garde theatrical improvisation pieces.

Another musical portrait is Wheel of Fortune (1969),
written for William O. Smith, a clarinet virtuoso and jazz
player.   Smith wears a quasi-Pierrot costume and is required to change hats several times.   In an interview published in the Seattle Times Smith described some of the actions that Oliveros specifies.   "The piece begins like a magic
ritual, and then the script tells me to 'tell the audience a
brief story about yourself in French' and then 'tell a little
known fact about Benny Goodman.'   And so on.   The piece
uses slides taken from the Tarot pack, some stuff on tape,
and my playing for two-to-five minutes of the 12-to-15 minutes piece."[3]   During the time that Smith actually plays the
clarinet he improvises using only six notes.

Sometimes Oliveros writes special improvisations for
accordion and voice that she performs herself.   They are
slowly changing drones forming a complex timbral mix between the accordion and voice.   There are no breaks or sudden changes in these pieces.   Instead the improvisations are
intense and the composer/performer communicates a harmo-
nious security between herself and the instrument and her
position as composer and improviser.   This kind of graceful
strength is frequently mentioned in interviews and articles
about Oliveros.

In 1967 Oliveros left San Francisco (her work at the
San Francisco Tape Music Center and Mills College is discussed in Chapter 4) to join the faculty of the University of
California at San Diego.   The Music Department was newly
established and interested in promoting Oliveros's expertise
with improvisation and electronic music.   She formed an
improvisation group of students and in 1969 began to work

with Al Huang, a dancer and practitioner of T'ai Chi. [4]
Oliveros would improvise with her accordion and voice during Huang's T'ai Chi sessions and occasionally invited other
musicians to join her. These experiences became material
for later compositions.

In addition to improvisation Oliveros states that her
work is related to primary process imagery, Sigmund
Freud's description of the deep primitive impulses that are
often revealed in dreams and other creative activities. She
began to keep a record of her dreams and to study them
seriously. Dreams would later influence her music, such
as her improvisations with voice and accordion. Oliveros's
improvisations increased her trust in her own creativity,
and she developed an inquisitiveness about aspects of her
personality that were being expressed in her compositions.
Sensitive to her emotions and general physical and psychological states, she used these efforts at self-understanding
as an impetus for her music. As a result she began to ignore the artistic boundaries of distance between the artist
and artwork, and her music became even more personal.

She voiced some of her feelings about the feminist
movement and the difficulties of the feminine spirit in trying
to express itself in a large piece, To Valerie Solanas and
Marilyn Monroe in Recognition of Their Desperation----
(1970). Howard Hirsch, director of the New Music Ensemble of the San Francisco Conservatory of Music, commissioned the piece. Hirsch performed the orchestra version,
but the first performance was with a small ensemble at
Hope College in September 1970. Oliveros played synthesizer.

The title is a dedication to two women who struggled
with their personal artistic expression. Valerie Solanas, a
young film actress, was so desperate that in 1968 she shot
and wounded Andy Warhol, and Marilyn Monroe was grossly
misunderstood and misrepresented. There is even doubt
that she deliberately committed suicide. [5]

To Valerie Solanas is calm and meditative. The
basic material is unmodulated and modulated long tones (probably an outcome of the cello drone in her Variations), improvised by any group or groups of instruments. The modulations are timbral changes that can be made while keeping
pitch constant, such as wind multiphonics, fluctuations in
bow pressure, vibrato, or changes of stops on an organ.
Before the performance each person selects five pitches,

two of which are nondiatonic or dissonant to the other three.
The pitches selected must be such that the fundamental can
be sustained while varying its overtone partials, amplitude,
and articulation.   This requires a sensitive person who has
both command of the instrument and experience with improvising timbres.

The piece, which can be performed in versions last-
ing thirty, forty-five, or sixty minutes, forms an arch of
three sections.   A lighting system gives timing cues and
also indicates changes in the use of material.

The score is a series of prose directions describing
the conductor's signals and telling the performers what to do.
Part 1 gradually introduces all five pitches from each player
so the listener has an opportunity to identify specific pitches
as characteristic of certain performers.   A lighting change
indicates when modulatory techniques are to be incorporated,
and the listener now begins to pay attention to changes in
qualities other than pitch.   Part 2 is a development because
one is to "steal pitches and modulation techniques from the
other players." Sometimes the robbery is not successful--
pitches may not be accurately matched and modulation techniques may differ among various instruments--but the real
challenge is recognizing and registering the successes.
Both audience and performers are involved in the same kind
of intensive listening necessary for dynamic improvisation.
Part 3 is a retrograde action returning to the beginning
pitches.

Oliveros describes To Valerie Solanas and Marilyn
Monroe in Recognition of Their Desperation---- as a "nonhierarchical relationship of the players." All members of
the ensemble are equal: there are no first chairs or con-
certmasters.   All are to blend together, and if one performer is too loud, then the ensemble must raise its dynamic
level.   Again, this means careful listening.   It eliminates
any temptation to perform virtuoso passages.   These conditions resonate Oliveros's belief that feminism should encourage, at the very least, an examination of stereotyped
patterns, in this case the structure and functions of an orchestra.

I have performed the piece and found that its use of
nonhierarchical relationships and improvisation are successful because the directions clearly state the role of control
and freedom.   In preparing a performance it becomes quite

evident that listening and concentration skills of each person
control freedom. For instance, in stealing pitches and mod-
ulating techniques the performer's ear becomes the criterion
for matching pitches and duplicating internal actions within a
sound. The better one's ear, the freer that person is to enter into the action of the piece.

It is successful for the audience, too. In contrast to
the Trio for Flute, Percussion, and String Bass, there are
no ambiguities about how to listen. Changes in lighting indicate changes in sonic material, and the conductor's actions
cause obvious additions and alterations in the sound. The
colored lights also suggest a sensitivity to the coloring of
the sound. The main problem for the audience is sustaining
the concentration necessary to understand what it is hearing.
This is the art of listening.

On December 3, 1979, the American Composers'
Orchestra honored Oliveros by performing To Valerie Solanas
at Lincoln Center. However, the program notes and review
in the New York Times printed some untrue and damaging
information about the composer's feminist philosophy. The
printed program notes stated that she was a member of the
Society for Cutting Up Men (SCUM), an organization founded
by Valerie Solanas of which Solanas is the only member.

A small xeroxed slip of paper stating that Pauline
Oliveros was not or never has been a member of SCUM was
inserted in the Lincoln Center brochure, but Donal Henahan,
the music editor of the New York Times, either did not see
the correction or chose to ignore it. His review on Tues-
day, December 4, 1979, perpetuated and elaborated on the
falsehood. Henahan wrote: "Miss Oliveros, a West Coast
composer of militant feminist inclinations, wanted to dramatize the lives of two women who she felt were exploited by
men. . . . Although the concept smacks of pop sociology, it
certainly might be a theatrically valid one. Miss Oliveros,
however, makes only the vaguest attempt to justify her elaborate title, offering instead a general plan, without notation,
that involved slowly shifting cues and improvisation, in hopes
that musical theater will result."[6]

Henahan totally misunderstood the piece. There is
nothing in the sounds themselves or the performance that
even begins to suggest musical theater, unless one interprets
the lighting to have implied meaning. There are no movements, costumes, or visuals--only a title that is a dedication.

It may be that Henahan reacted to the title's four dashes and felt that he could supply further meaning to what the words actually said.   He also misunderstood the concept of improvisation and drone, implying that staff notation was the criterion for respectable music.

On December 12, 1979, Oliveros wrote the following letter to Henahan in defense of her music, her reputation, and good criticism in general.   This letter is included with permission of its author for documentation purposes.

December 12, 1979

Donal Henahan
Music Editor
The New York Times
229 West 43rd Street
New York, NY

To Donal Henahan in Recognition of His Desperation

Dear Mr. Henahan,

First of all I want to congratulate you on your presence at the concert Dec. 3, 1979 by the American Composer's Orchestra at Alice Tully Hall and your subsequent review which appeared in the New York Times Dec. 4, 1979. I believe that one of the important tasks of the music critic, no matter what his or her opinion of the music may be, is to acknowledge the activities of composers of our time.

Secondly, I want to thank you for devoting so much of your review to my work, although I feel that my colleagues could have received equal attention.

Thirdly, I would like to answer your criticism and hopefully clear some misconceptions on your part about my work and philosophy:
First, obviously, the composer is an organizer of musical material. Today musical material ranges through the whole spectrum of audible sound and is not limited to tones of a so-called periodic nature. Therefore standard western notation can be a limiting factor to a composer. Staff notation is not the only way that musical ideas can be understood or notated. The composer must choose the most appropriate way to notate or transmit the music. Notation may consist of any kind of graphic configurations, i.e. numbers, drawings, pictures, etc., or words as long as it effectively communicates to musicians.
Second, a major part of the world's music is not <u>written</u>, but is transmitted by oral tradition, or words and actions. Thus your opening statement about <u>writing</u> a piece of music versus offering a few guidelines or <u>sign</u> posts could stand considerable re-examination in the light of the total history of music, not just the past 20 years. It may be true that there is "less

of this practice" in Alice Tully Hall, but it is certainly an
important and indeed a most necessary "bright idea" in the
music world today. Your underlying sarcasm seems to spring, perhaps, from a wrong conception of what constitutes appropriate
musical notation.

The correct title of my piece is To Valerie Solanas and Marilyn
Monroe in Recognition of their Desperation -- not For Valerie
Solanas and Marilyn Monroe in Recognition of their Desperation.
This is a small detail, incorrect in the program, which could
cause confusion. The title, as stated in the program notes is
a dedication. It needs no justification. It was not intended
to imply theater on stage, or dramatize lives, as you so mis-
takenly assumed, but rather it is intended to stimulate the
listener. And what is wrong with an "elaborate title" especially if it provokes at least some kind of thought if not theater
on the stage? To is different from For. In my mind the piece
is directed to these women whose commonality was the desire to
be heard and understood in terms of their inner needs as artists.
The piece was not for their actions of desperation, suicide and
attempted murder, but "in recognition of their desperation" in
a society which was not listening to them, but forcefully imposing conceptions, which prevented their self-expression, finally leading to their anti-social acts. I fail to understand your
reference here to "Pop Sociology".

When I saw myself described as "a composer of militant feminist
inclinations", I was surprised that you would resort to a jour-
nalistic epithet. Perhaps you did not see the program note correction. Perhaps you believed the erroneous statement in the
program notes that I belonged to SCUM (The Society For Cutting
Up Men). I was not consulted on the final version of those
notes and I cannot imagine the origin of such an assumption.
I would be more likely to belong to the Society For Cutting Up
With Men. In any case the core of my feminist philosophy is
based on those social energies and directions which are beneficial for all living beings. It is my greatest desire that my
actions as an individual and a member of society, both local and
global, will spring from this principle which I call feminist.
Thus your epithet is inappropriate. I am a feminist if the
term implies the above principle but militant does not apply.

Your description of what the orchestra did is incomplete and
rather distorted. Here again the program notes give such inaccuracies as "Colored lights supply cues for individual pitches"
The lights provide cues for change in the accessibility of material. The pitches are supplied by the players. The players
know what pitches to play because they have chosen them prior
to the beginning of the piece according to specific guideline.
Naturally a perusal of the score could clear up such wrong no-
tions so please accept the enclosed score with my compliments.

You state "the improvised sound they created, while occasionally interesting as random antiphony, added up to half an hour of
droning, somewhat in the style of Ligeti's music for 2001: A
Space Odyssey, or any of 100 1960's exercises in static monotony."
A careful look at the score will show that your use of the term
improvise needs qualification. Certainly the players are engaged in a kind of improvisation, however, they are asked to do
this within rather strict guidelines. Your compliment concerning "occasionally interesting random antiphony" is questionable.
What is random antiphony? Random, it is well-known, has a large
range and also needs qualification. What is random about three

groups in a specified spatial relationship consciously choosing when, what and how to play, again according to guidelines? As for droning in the style of Ligeti, I am glad to be in such good company even though our esthetics are miles apart and neither piece would stand analysis as a drone; there are too many structural changes. Incidentally, where can I find 100 1960's exercises in "static monotony"? Do you mean _ecstatic_ monotony? Actually every piece of music is static or monotonous in some respect or else one would not be able to discern any form. Perhaps you mean unity, after all "static monotony" could be understood as redundant if not sloppy writing.

You say that "In view of the evangelical nature of the Oliveros work, it was odd that all three of the conductors who controlled the proceedings were males." I hardly consider myself evangelical. I don't consider it odd that the three conductors were male. Isn't that usually the case? The piece has been conducted by three women recently in Boston. It seems only fair to have equal representation in this performance especially with men who were so sensitive and feminist in their outlook. I don't recall ever being reviewed by a woman in the New York Times. What about that? Never the less, the conductors don't totally "control the proceedings" but interact with the musicians sometimes controlling sometimes just listening and accepting. Again you impose a concept which is not appropriate and could be cleared up by looking at the score.

What would be far more interesting to me than your attempted description and judgement, is a description of your real feelings as you listened to my piece. How do you account for the warm reception given to me by the audience? How do you account for the fact that my box overflowed with friends and people, during and after the intermission, giving me warm congratulations and thanks for the experience?

Although it wasn't perfect, I was happy with the performance. The players were generally sensitive and cooperative. The occasion was only spoiled for me by my distress over the program notes with those erroneous assumptions and possible consequences such as were reflected in your review.

In conclusion, I have written to you in the interests of communication and in hopes of closing the gap which exists between composers and their critics. Because the issues raised in this letter are so important to me, I intend to make this an open letter to all who may be concerned.

I wish you a good future as a critic of good new music.

Sincerely yours,

Pauline Oliveros

Pauline Oliveros

PO\ac

Further research revealed the true cause of the falsehood that Oliveros belongs to SCUM. The entry about Oliveros in Baker's Biographical Dictionary, both the 1971 sup-
plement and sixth edition, states that she is a member of
SCUM and makes many other errors about her work. [7] Apparently it was assumed that since a piece was dedicated to
Valerie Solanas, then Oliveros must also be a member of
Solanas's "organization." Baker's, edited by Nicolas Slonimsky, is considered a reputable source of information and
was used as reference material in preparing the program
notes for Lincoln Center.

Anyone who has heard Oliveros's music, attended one
of her lectures, or read articles by her or about her work,
would observe that she is a nonmilitant and nonviolent person. Oliveros bears no ill feelings toward men, nor does
she want to seek revenge for the male domination of women.
In an interview by Elinor Kefalas published in the Musical
America section of High Fidelity/Musical America Oliveros described the problems of her career as a woman
composer as being resistance within her own self: obstacles
that she created. [8]

The inaccuracies of the Baker's entry and the distorted review in the New York Times are examples of how
often creative work produced by women is not considered to
be serious, or is at least suspect. Oliveros experienced
this problem numerous times and even discussed it in her
article "And Don't Call Them Lady Composers," published
in the New York Times, September 13, 1970. She advised
critics that they should be more observant of their language
patterns and pay more attention to the work of women composers. In an address to the National Convention of the
American Society of University Composers, held at the
University of Cincinnati in April 1981, she enlarged this
concern, making it applicable to male and female composers and offered some practical solutions to the problem of
adequate criticism of new music.

Critics, too, often misunderstand improvisation as
weak and lacking technical compositional skills. Notation is
the cause of this problem, as Oliveros so candidly explained
to Henahan. All too often a piece of music is judged by the
visual impression of the score, where multiple staves, leg-
ends, footnotes, arrows, circles, and other marks of the
draftsman's trade become the criteria of a composition's
quality.

After the <u>Outline for Flute, Percussion, and String
Bass</u> Oliveros completely abandoned standard notation and
began to experiment with simple directions that tell performers what to do and how to listen.   Her contribution to John
Cage's published collection of music manuscripts, <u>Notations,</u>
is the first page of her <u>Pieces of Eight</u> (1964), an early work
in her prose notational style.   See Example 12.   Notice the
handwritten directions telling exactly what is to be done and
the edited sentence "Listen to the clock ticking."[9]

Improvisation and composing directions for improvisation are skills that must be practiced, and Oliveros included
these as part of her teaching techniques.   She frequently de-
vised improvisation exercises to develop ear-training and
basic musicianship skills.   One of these exercises became
the basis for <u>Willowbrook Generations and Reflections</u> (1976),
commissioned by the Willowbrook High School Band, Donald
De Roche, conductor.   The work is for mixed winds, brasses, and voices (twenty or more) or chorus alone.

Although composed in 1976, <u>Willowbrook Generations
and Reflections</u> resembles <u>To Valerie Solanas.</u>   Both pieces
are adaptable.   Time, space, and the number of performers
depend upon the occasion and resources.   The players' primary responsibility in <u>Willowbrook</u> is short reaction time in
matching pitch.   Conductors (two are needed) have more control of the improvisation than in <u>To Valerie Solanas,</u> probably because the commission was for young musicians.   The
composition demands utmost concentration from the performers.   They must constantly pay attention to a conductor,
listen, and match pitch in as short a reaction time as possible.

The entire ensemble is divided into two groups: a
Generating Group and a Reflecting Group.   The figure on
page 48 shows how the performers are to be arranged in a
gymnasium.   (There is an alternate stage version.)

Members of the Generating Group are paired in terms
of like instruments or instruments with a pitch and dynamic
range in common.   When cued by a conductor, the person
plays a short clear pitch, which the partner must immediately duplicate.

The Reflecting Group reinforces and adds long decays
to the improvised pitches.   This group is arranged so that
their sounds surround the audience.   If space permits, some

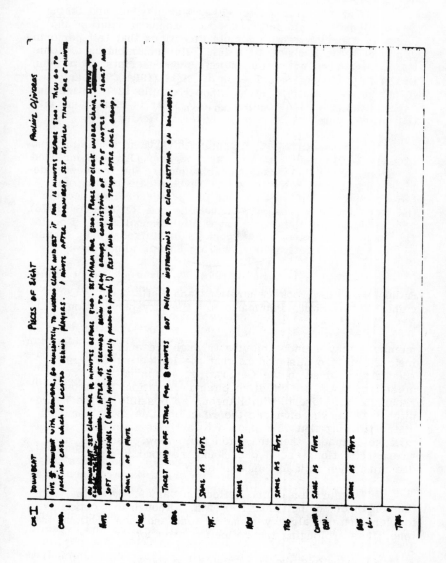

Example 12.   Pieces of Eight, in Notations, edited by John
Cage.   Used by permission.

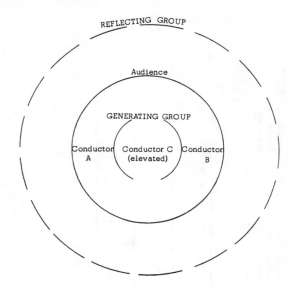

Setup for <u>Willowbrook Generations and Reflections</u>.   Copyright 1977 by Smith Publications.   Used by permission.

members may even be moving through the audience.   The instructions are designed so that the Reflecting Groups' sounds are joined to the Generating Groups' attack.   The musicians must use intuitive pitch recognition; the attack should be as close to simultaneous as possible to the heard pitch.   Oliveros considers the reaction time to be the core of the training that is supposed to activate intuition.   If a mistake is made, then the pitch must slowly fade out as a wrong reflection, and if one cannot respond immediately, one must then wait for another pitch.

The duration of the reflection varies, depending upon the length of an individual's breath, although one option is to blend into an already-sounding tone and then continue that tone, thus prolonging the reflection even longer.

Conductors are responsible for the action, which is to resemble "the organic rhythm of a natural environment such as a forest."   Their listening, concentration abilities, and reaction time are crucial to the piece's success, just as the performers' pitch recognition generates and reflects the material.   The score states:

> The conductors must remain aware of the conse-
> quences of their cues for each other as well as
> the Generating Group and Reflecting Group....
> Conductors A and B sense these reflections, some-
> times listening for them to die away or thin out
> before generating new pitches by cueing players,
> sometimes cueing new pitches quickly or in rapid
> flurries so that reflections may overlap and accu-
> mulate. The result should be long slow chords
> from the Reflecting Group and voices, sometimes
> thick, sometimes thin, which slowly sweep the
> performance space as different players join the
> prolongations or release, the short pitches sound-
> ing like punctuation. 10

Oliveros was sensitive to the situation in which the
audience consisted of friends and parents wanting to know
what the young musicians were playing, so she included a
prelude to the performance. Conductors and some performers demonstrate how the directions work so that the
audience realizes the challenging gamelike nature of Willowbrook Generations and Reflections. Also, the audience is
invited to reinforce the reflections vocally if anyone wants
to participate in the piece.

Notes

1. Oliveros writes about these experiences in an unpublished manuscript about her theater pieces.

2. San Francisco Chronicle, March 26, 1962.

3. Seattle Times, October 11, 1970.

4. For more information about T'ai Chi see Al Chung-liang
Huang, Embrace Tiger, Return to Mountain (New York:
Bantam, 1974).

5. Edward Charles Wagenknecht, Marilyn Monroe: A Composite View (Philadelphia: Chilton, 1969).

6. For another critic's opinion of this performance see
Tom Johnson's review in the Village Voice, December 17,
1979.

7.   Baker's Biographical Dictionary, 6th ed., completely revised by Nicolas Slonimsky (New York: Schirmer, 1978), pp. 1259-1260.

8.   Elinor Kefalas, "Pauline Oliveros: An Interview," High Fidelity/Musical America, June 1975, pp. MA24-25.

9.   John Cage, Notations (West Glover, Vt.:   Something Else Press, 1969, unp.).

10.   Willowbrook Generations and Reflections is published by Smith Publications.

4: ELECTRONIC MUSIC

The early 1960s was a challenging era for Oliveros. She had used her Gaudeamus prize money for a short European trip and returned to San Francisco eager to continue her work. She was receiving recognition as the composer of the post-Webern-style Variations and Trio for Flute, Piano and Page Turner but was also establishing a reputation as a daring experimenter in improvisation with mixed media and electronics.

Oliveros had been recording sounds since 1948, when her mother purchased an early-model wire recorder, a predecessor of the tape recorder. Naturally Oliveros experimented with this machine, but one day a tape recorder taught her a lesson about listening that affected the future direction of her work. She put a microphone in the window of her San Francisco apartment and recorded the environment. Later, when listening to the results, she was astonished to realize that there were many sounds she had never noticed, and decided that she would try to be always aware of sound, considering the environment as a continual symphony. From that time on the microphone was a supersensitive ear and the tape recorder was an extension of her sonic memory. These instruments made her acutely aware of listening skills.

As a child Oliveros was fond of listening to what was then considered nonmusical material. She reports:

> Sometimes during the mid 1930's I used to listen to my grandfather's crystal radio over earphones. I loved the crackling

static. The same grandfather used to try to teach
me the Morse Code with telegraph keys. I wasn't
interested in the messages but I loved the dit da
dit dit rhythms. I used to spend a lot of time
tuning my father's radio, especially to the whistles
and white noise between the stations. I loved the
peculiar acoustical phenomena which involved my
parents' voices on long rides in the car. I would
lie in the back seat listening intently to the modulation resultants produced by voices interacting
with engine vibration. I didn't care what they
were saying. I also loved our wind-up Victrola,
especially when the mechanism was running down
with a record playing. I loved all the negative
operant phenomena of systems. [1]

Her first electronic composition, Time Perspectives
(1961), was a concrete tape piece using recorded environmental sounds realized on her Silvertone Sears and Roebuck
home tape recorder. She enhanced the quality of her concrete tape by rerecording it in her bathroom, which was
equipped with cardboard tube filters and an especially resonant bathtub, a practical solution to the lack of a studio.

Locating equipment was a crucial problem during
those beginning years of electronic music. The group Sonics
had managed to gather some essentials for the San Francisco
Conservatory's modest electronic music studio. While Oliveros was in Europe Ramon Sender and Morton Subotnick,
who at that time taught at Mills College in Oakland and was
the musical director of Ann Halprin's Dancers' Workshop in
San Francisco, decided to pool resources and form a group
that they called the San Francisco Tape Music Center. Oliveros joined the group after she returned from Europe. In
her words, "They begged, borrowed, and stole equipment."[2]
One historic outcome was their collaboration with Donald
Buchla, then a young electrical engineer, in developing a
synthesizer now known as the Buchla Electronic Music Box.

At first the studio was located in an old condemned
house, but the San Francisco Tape Music Center eventually
joined with the Dancers' Workshop, KPFA, and Canyon Cine-
ma and moved to 321 Divisadero Street. The building was
ideal. A large upstairs room was used as a performance
space where dancers, musicians, and other artists collaborated in producing monthly concerts. The proceeds paid
the rent. Many musicians visiting the West Coast stopped

Members of the San Francisco Tape Music Center: Ramon
Sender, Michael Callahan, Pauline Oliveros, and Anthony
Martin

to see and use the Tape Center.   Even some famous pre-
miers occurred there, such as Terry Riely's In C (1964).
For a time KPFA set up a studio in one of the small rooms
so that it could broadcast concerts.

In 1965 the Center received funding from the Rockefeller Foundation.   The grant stipulated that the Center re-
locate so that funds could be properly administered.   It
moved to Mills College.   Subotnick, who had been on the
Mills faculty, was leaving the West Coast, so Oliveros was
made director of the San Francisco Tape Music Center at
its new location.

Oliveros's catalog of tape pieces, montages of electronic sounds mixed with acoustical and prerecorded material, and collaborations with the Dancers' Workshop and others
is extensive.   Since she lists every piece and activity in her
catalog (see especially the years 1965-66, page 153, below),
I have selected a few of her most outstanding electronic compositions as examples of her work in this area.

Bye Bye Butterfly (1965), available on "New Music
for Electronic and Recorded Media" (1750 Arch Records

S-1765), is a recent recorded release of Oliveros's work, although it is an example of her early interest in tape delay, a technique she used in most of her electronic music. Tape delay is a simple process that can yield sophisticated sonic results.   Some home tape recorders have switches that permit a tape-delay configuration, but more complicated effects can be achieved by using two or more machines. The basic principle is the reiteration or echo of feedback. Material being recorded on one machine is simultaneously threaded through another tape recorder that is in the playback mode, and then the output is routed back to the first tape recorder so that the initial machine is recording its current material and also the sound of past material.   The time delay between a sound and its repetition depends upon the distance between the two tape recorders. [3]

Tape delay

One of the results of tape delay is a reverberant sound resembling live sound heard in a favorable acoustic environment.   This quality was crucial, since one of the major criticisms of early electronic music was that it sounded dead or static.   The sounds were so perfect that they lacked the transient activity of acoustical sound that we now recognize as part of the listening pleasure.

The beauty of tape delay, and one reason why Oliveros used it, is that it does not require a large amount of equipment.   The tape recorder itself is used as the medium to modulate and transform sound.   Changes in timbre, texture, and intensity occur when sounds are instantly replayed and mixed with new incoming material.   The amplitude or volume of the reverberated tape delay must be carefully controlled because the echo will continually feed upon itself and become so loud that it obliterates other sounds.   Sudden increases in volume result in gross changes in sound.   Adding a mixer to control which inputs are being recorded and repeated makes it possible to select and or discard developing sonic events.

Another attractive feature of tape delay is that it is especially appropriate for real-time performance. Sound sources for the tape delay can be prearranged. For example, oscillators or mixers could be available, or acoustical sounds occurring at the time of performance can be amplified and used as sound sources. Oliveros was particularly sensitive to both of these situations. Her previous work in improvisation was a good preparation for the listening and remembering that is necessary when using tape delay.

The difficulties of tape delay are trying to avoid the clichés of repeated sound and the rapid buildup of unwanted material. The success of the process depends upon a musical sense of time (knowing when to make changes and when to allow events to develop naturally) and a musical ear (recognizing how sounds are presently interacting and predicting what changes will occur in the very near future, sometimes one or two seconds later). This is one reason why tape-delay setups are usually a solo performance. These instant decisions are unpredictable and are best controlled by one person.

Bye Bye Butterfly is an easy piece to understand and an elegant listening experience that has been called "one of the most beautiful pieces of electronic music to emerge from the 60's."4

There are two basic sounds to the piece: an extremely high and narrow band of white noise resembling radio static (and if one listens closely, there is a corresponding low band of static, too) and a section of Giacomo Puccini's opera Madame Butterfly (1904). Surprisingly, the piece begins with an annoying click, but then what sounds like white noise is modulated and shaped by the tape delay. After three minutes there is an abrupt entrance of recognizable operatic music that is continually laced with changing lines of static. The piece is a marvelous example of electronic counterpoint, since the repetition of the tape delay causes reverberation and modulation of the segment from Butterfly. It is as if one is hearing distorted mirrors. At times Madame Butterfly sounds like a reverberating melismatic chorus of herself, and Puccini's music assumes a complexity that is lacking in the original. The section that Oliveros used begins with the Lentamente of Act II, Part I (page 193 in the Ricordi piano vocal score) and ends at the cadence to the Meno ♩ = 69 (page 214). The beginning measures, where one first recognizes the Puccini material, are shown in Example 13.

Example 13.   Beginning measures of <u>Lentamente</u> from <u>Madame Butterfly</u>.   Copyright 1904, 1907, and 1954 by G. Ricordi and Co.   Used by permission of Associated Music Publishers, Inc.

    The operatic action is at the point where Butterfly and Suzuki, her maid, are anticipating the return of Pinkerton, Butterfly's American husband, and the two women are decorating the room with flowers.   Puccini used this scene in his opera to ease tension.   The music is light and melodic in order to form a contrast for the final part, where Butterfly realizes she has been deceived and commits suicide.

    But Oliveros's distorted version of <u>Butterfly</u> is not light and melodic at all.   Her <u>Butterfly</u> sounds surrealistic since the listener is forced to follow the angular melody of the static and reverberated interference rather than the familiar curves of the original.   The actual material of the opera is hardly distinct.   The descending third from F^5 to Db^5 in the vocal line and the augmented chords in the accompaniment (see circled items in Example 13) are clearly heard in Oliveros's <u>Butterfly</u> and then become repeated and juxtaposed upon other material.   Listeners know that somewhere Butterfly is singing, but what is being heard is a complete transformation of the original.

    Part of the appeal of <u>Bye Bye Butterfly</u> is its ternary form and comfortable listening time of eight minutes.   The A section begins with tape-delayed electronic sounds; the B section features the entrance and modulation of <u>Madame Butterfly</u>; and the final A section returns to the electronic sounds and continues the tape-delay process.

    The basic sonic gestures also create a sense of formal

unity. The tape-delay technique and the frequency modulation produce wavelike gestures resembling sonic good-byes to Butterfly. This imagery continues as the real <u>Butterfly</u> shifts from being in focus to out of focus, depending upon the amount of overlay.

There is one last point about the structure and process of how <u>Bye Bye Butterfly</u> was improvised. The annoying click at the beginning of the piece sounds like a bad splice, but Oliveros is far too careful to allow such a noise unless she has a definite purpose for it. The sound is actually the click produced when she turned on the turntable at the beginning of the piece. Since she had the volume reduced, <u>Butterfly</u> was not heard until later, but the record was playing during the entire duration of <u>Bye Bye Butterfly</u>. Curiously, there is another click heard and repeated as tape delay immediately before <u>Butterfly</u> becomes audible. This click adds a percussive motive to the texture and is the result of turning up the volume of the mixer so that the real <u>Butterfly</u> can be heard. These details illustrate Oliveros's improvisatory skills. Clicks are usually undesirable but often unavoidable in a real-time performance, so she incorporated them as part of the musical texture.

In the summer of 1966 Oliveros left San Francisco and went to Toronto to study with Hugh Le Caine, who was known for his inventive work using touch-sensitive keyboard devices for electronic music. Although Oliveros stayed at the studio for only two months, she was active in producing the following tapes: <u>5000 Miles</u>, <u>I of IV</u>, <u>II of IV</u>, <u>III of IV</u>, <u>IV of IV</u>, <u>The Day I Disconnected the Erase Head</u> and <u>Forgot to Reconnect It</u>, <u>Big Mother Is Watching You</u>, <u>NO MO</u>, <u>Participle Dangling in Honor of Gertrude Stein</u> (mobile, film, and tape), <u>Ultra Sonic Studies in Real Time</u> (two tapes), and six additional ultrasonic studies.[5]

Her primary interest was employing tape-delay techniques with experiments using amplified combination tones that she had made in San Francisco. Combination tones are sometimes heard when two or more tones are sounding simultaneously. This phenomenon had interested her for quite some time: "When I was sixteen, my accordion teacher taught me to hear combination tones. The accordion is particularly able to produce them if you squeeze hard enough. From that time, I wished for a way to eliminate the fundamental tones so I could listen only to the combination tones. When I was thirty-two, I began to set signal generators

beyond the range of hearing and to make electronic music
from amplified combination tones.   I felt like a witch cap-
turing sounds from a nether realm. "[6]

Musicians who play acoustic instruments frequently
do not pay attention to these combination tones or even to
the overtone structure of the sounds that their instruments
produce. Either the pitch is changing so rapidly or these
combination tones decay so quickly that there is not enough
time to listen carefully to the structure of the sounds.   It
was the advent of electronic music that brought full attention to the resources of these combination tones. [7]

In 1966 Oliveros was pioneering work with combination tones and expanded her projects to include subaudio and
supersonic frequencies. Since she wanted to eliminate the
fundamentals, she worked with sound sources that were
above and below the range of human hearing. If two oscillators are tuned to supersonic frequencies and their output is properly amplified, then the sounds heard are the
difference tones produced by the unheard fundamentals. The
difference tone (another aspect of combination tones) will be
a frequency that is the difference in frequency of the two
originals.   Therefore the heard difference tone of the supersonic fundamentals will be a lower pitch.

The subaudio oscillator, again if properly amplified,
could produce frequency modulation and cause changes in the
frequencies of the supersonic oscillators by disturbing their
wave pattern.   Actually subaudio oscillators have been used
since the 1930s to produce a vibrato in electronic organs.
Anyone familiar with a Hammond organ knows the wide range
of vibrato rates that can be selected.

But using subaudio and supersonic frequencies was so
new to electronic music that apparently some people in the
studio found Oliveros's work threatening. In her article
"Some Sound Observations" she recollects:

> In one electronic studio I was accused of
> black art, and the director disconnected one ampli-
> fier to discourage my practices, declaring that
> signal generators are of no use above or below
> the audio range because you can't hear them.
> Since all processing equipment contains amplifiers,
> I found that I could cascade two pieces of equip-
> ment and get enough gain for my combination tones

to continue my work, plus the addition of various amplifier characteristics or orchestration. I worked there for two months, and for recreation, would ride my bicycle to the town power plant where I would listen for hours to the source of my newly-found powers. 8

The results of this experience turned out to be beneficial. I of IV, a tape she made at the Toronto Studio using the techniques described above, was recorded on "Music of Our Times" (Odyssey 32 16 0160). I of IV uses the familiar sounds of electronic drones, long sustaining buzzing and humming sounds. The piece lasts almost twenty-one minutes, but it is well organized into four sections and like Bye Bye Butterfly is a real-time improvisation featuring tape delay. Oliveros, however, used a double feedback loop for I of IV, one that permitted more control and a greater range of changes of timbre and intensity. 9

As part of my research I went to a power plant, the source of entertainment for Oliveros while in Toronto, and just listened. The plant emits an audible complex drone based upon the 60-cycle hum of electricity. It is a technological sound familiar to every household as the refrigerator's hum, the sound of the blender, hair dryer, and so on. While concentrating on the sound, I was able to distinguish overtones of a fifth, third, and other higher and sometimes unidentifiable pitches. The more I listened, the more I heard. Although the outer range of the drone was stable, I perceived its inner activity as constantly changing. There was a characteristic reverberant pulse, and the environment affected how I heard the drone. If I walked around the plant, my perception was altered: new pitches were audible and other areas of sound seemed to be absorbed by surrounding trees.

Suddenly I realized that I was hearing the sound and activity of I of IV and that I of IV was a statement about the nature of electricity, the very medium of electronic music. Certain other aspects of the piece also supported this idea.

First, it was appropriate that I of IV was an improvisation since electronic drones are always present, and I of IV captured twenty-one minutes of this electrical reality. Second, certain musical elements of the piece support the position that it is a statement about the nature of electricity.

The improvisation follows a traditional tonal formal scheme caused by Oliveros's manipulation of the drones and what sounds she allowed to be heard in the tape-delay process.   This is immediately apparent to the listener because the twenty-one minutes are divided into four sections that resemble an exposition, development, recapitulation, and coda.   The temporal proportions of these sections, similar to a sonata-allegro design, are illustrated below.

```
0---------5:30'------9:30'-----------17'------21'
```

EXPO-	DEVEL-	RECAPITU-	CODA
SITION	OPMENT	LATION	

Temporal proportions in I of IV

The expository nature of section I becomes evident as a strong and steady C^4 drone emerges amid other harmonically complex sonic activity.   Bits and fragments of higher frequencies are heard, but their duration is so short that the listener is only momentarily exposed to this upper sonic world.   It is as if small windows are quickly opened and shut so that only snatches of existing sounds are evident, but one has the sense that the composer is definitely in control of these sounds and when they will be heard.   Musically this section could be interpreted as a tuning of both listener and performer to the resources of the piece.

Gradually Oliveros exposes more of the sonic activity. The feedback process temporarily accumulates and subsides to reveal transforming qualities of the tape delay.   The double feedback loop becomes apparent because there are several different rates of attack and delay, a long eight-second delay and other shorter ones.   The drone's intensity diminishes, and the interval of a minor third begins to be prominent, especially the repeated movement C♯ to A♯. The timbre of the drone is both the same and constantly changing.   A reinforcement at the upper register presents a purer timbre, and then, as one listens closely, the pitch of that timbre is microtonal.   Gradually one notices an eight-second ostinato (the result of the tape delay).   The predictability of this situation could be deadly, but Oliveros carefully controls her feedback process.   The counterpoint of the repeated material is always distinguishable, not blurred by unwanted and quickly accumulating reiteration.

The changes in timbre, texture, and intensity are subtly
controlled in the composition, almost to the point where the
listener would like to hear more.

Section II presents a contrast to the preceding events.
By now the strong presence of C^4 disappears and a modulation takes place. $F\sharp^4$ gradually emerges as the tonal center
and the process of tape delay becomes more active as various chords and minor sixths predominate. The texture
thickens and complex sound masses in the lower registers
are more noticeable.

The third section leads directly out of this texture
into a thinner and lighter one featuring short attacks of constantly changing minor thirds. The feeling and mood shifts
from the heaviness of the accumulated sounds in the previous
section to a light scherzo feeling. Eventually $F\sharp$ emerges
and gradually an $A\sharp$ drone appears and is counterpointed
against the $F\sharp$ forming a drone duet of alternating attacks,
but then a distinct A is heard and short glissandi decorate
the texture and begin to disturb the drones. This causes a
conflict in the tonal scheme. The original C^4 of section I
returns as part of an $E\flat$-C gesture, but it is in competition
with a throbbing $F\sharp$. The tape delay's activity increases,
and one expects the performance to end with a flurry, but a
new section that functions as a coda emerges. The tonal
center clearly supports $F\sharp$ with occasional short drones on
other pitches, and then suddenly I of IV ends with an unexpected and clear articulation of $F\sharp^6$ to B^6.

But Oliveros did not intend that this event would end
the piece. The original tape is slightly longer than the
twenty-one-minute record format; the ending on the record
sounds convincing, however, and shows how traditional musical patterns were subtly functioning as part of the improvisation with an electronic medium. In fact I hear Oliveros's
electronic music as more tonally oriented than her earlier
acoustic music, and in 1969 she began to experiment with
single-pitch pieces, such as A-OK (1969) and Music for Expo
'70 (1970).

This curious perfect authentic cadence at the end of
I of IV is a clue to the understanding of the piece. One
may wonder about the validity of a tonal analysis, but I suggest that it is the key to the piece's structure and supports
the position that I of IV is a statement about the very nature
of electricity. The motivic imprint of the thirds (especially

the minor thirds) and the absence of strong intervals of the
fourth or fifth (except at the final cadence) indicate that
these drones are composed of the upper partials of an overtone series, and all of this activity is taking place in a
realm where one can not hear the fundamental.   This is
exactly what Oliveros wanted to do: force the listener to
hear the upper partials and combination tones while ignor-
ing the fundamentals.   That octave reinforcement (heard especially in section II) causes microtonal shifting also shows
that these sounds are related to a fundamental well below
our range of hearing, since the sounds heard are in the upper microtonal range of the partial series.   Supposing that
this fundamental is a low 7.5 cycles per second and equat-
ing 60 cycles per second as a quasi B in our equal-tempered
tuning system, then the following overtone structure is produced.   The circled pitches in Example 14 are the prominent drone tones in I of IV and show how I of IV is tuned
to the pitch of electricity used in the United States and
Canada.

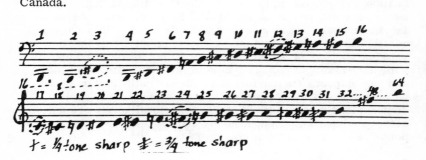

$+$ = ¼ tone sharp $\ddagger$ = ¾ tone sharp

Example 14.   Overtone structure produced by the B of 7.5
cycles per second

It is the final cadence that reveals the source of sonic
activity, but actually the clue is also in the title.   The last
sound heard, B, is the tonic (I) of the four (IV) sections.
Functionally the primary drones of C and F♯ work as the
upper leading tone (Neapolitan) and dominant of B.   See the
circled pitches in Example 14.   The earlier observation that
I of IV was really a statement about the nature of electricity
is supported by the fact that the piece is an exposition of
the upper overtones related to the 60-cycle hum.   It is appropriate that these sounds are really produced by the combination tones resulting from supersonic realms.

An additional appropriateness is the modifying agent of the double tape delay. The synthesis of the texture, timbre, and dynamics is produced by the two tape recorders (electronic instruments), Oliveros, as master controller, decided when and how much should be heard.

Equally fitting is that these decisions produced a strong and coherent form. Oliveros is an accomplished improviser and able to incorporate traditional patterns and structures intuitively during real-time performance.

This type of all-inclusive listening combined with the use of electronics became the basis for another piece, In Memoriam Nikola Tesla, Cosmic Engineer (1969), which Oliveros composed as a commission from the Merce Cunningham Foundation. The piece became the musical score for Cunningham's dance "Canfield" and won the Grand Prix at the Belgrade International Theater Festival in 1972. The score was inspired by J. J. O'Neill's biography of Nikola Tesla, the electrical engineering genius who discovered the theory of alternating current (which he later sold to George Westinghouse). 10

Oliveros considers "Canfield" a type of solitaire in which Cunningham used ideas from the biography of Tesla for the choreography, and Robert Morris designed a set that included a lighting batten in front of the stage. But the music, set, and dance were independently conceived.

Oliveros was especially interested in Tesla's experiment with mechanical resonance. 11 In 1896 Tesla was studying high-frequency electrical oscillations and also experimenting with mechanical vibrations. He fastened his mechanical electrical oscillator to an iron supporting pillar in the middle of his New York City laboratory and observed how various objects shook and sounded as the oscillator came in tune with their individual resonant frequencies. Tesla did not know that these vibrations were being transmitted through the building's columns to the gound and were causing minor earthquakes in the neighborhood. But suddenly he realized that he was about to destroy his laboratory; the oscillator was rapidly approaching the resonant frequency of the building and would literally shake the structure to pieces. Tesla took a sledgehammer, destroyed the oscillator, and saved the building.

Tesla's experiment gave Oliveros the idea for her

score. She required that musicians recreate Tesla's search
and try to discover the resonant frequency of the theater
where the dance is being performed. The score involves
recording a discussion about testing the space and, finally,
a sounding via audio generators of the supposed discovered
resonant frequency. Oliveros says: "If the search for the
resonant frequency has been successful, then the frequency
of the generators selected by the musicians can cause the
performance space to add its squeaks, groans, and other
resonance phenomena to the general sounds. Thus the space
performs in sympathy with the musicians."[12] Again Oliveros
adopts electronics as part of an improvisation using active
listening to generate and control sonic feedback.

Not long after writing In Memoriam Nikola Tesla,
Oliveros was asked to submit a proposal for live programming for the Pepsi-Cola Pavilion that was being planned for
the Expo '70 to be held in Osaka, Japan. The Pavilion
project was a unique collaboration between artists and in-
dustry. The concept was that the visitors should participate and involve themselves in both the technological hard-
ware and the artistic experience. David Tudor, working
with the organization Experiments in Art and Technology,
with which Pepsi-Cola had contracted for their Pavilion
project, was responsible for the sound system. He wanted
the sound to travel throughout the performance space. His
original idea was to have twenty separate channels, loudspeakers mounted on multiple grids, and a digital console
that would control the spatial path of the sound. The idea
was too elaborate, and the design was modified and limited
to only five speakers.

Oliveros submitted A-OK (1969), an improvisation
piece using tape delay, four loudspeakers, and live musicians, to the Pavilion committee. The piece is for violin-
ists, a chorus, conductors, and accordionist (Oliveros was
the performer), who create drones, chants, and occasional
melodic patterns based upon an A tonality. Suspended micro-
phones picked up the sound, which was then modified by the
tape delay, played back, and further mixed with the live
sounds. The visual elements of A-OK were a lighting system, revolving platform, and a circular rotation of the performers.

Oliveros prepared a tape, Pep-Psi (also called Music
for Expo '70), which was another drone improvised by voices,
accordion, and two celli. Oliveros controlled the tonality of

the improvisation and used the Pavilion's dome to add acoustical interest to the sound of the tape. The tape was played while hostesses sang with it and guided visitors in exploring the sound-reflective qualities of the Pavilion's dome. 13

By the mid 1970s Oliveros was an experienced teacher of electronic music. As a student in one of her classes I was able to observe her attitudes and techniques. Her practical nature was evident in the way that she worked with the equipment and taught the class.

Our first assignment was to diagram the studio, indicating the various modules and labeling their inputs and outputs and other configurations. The diagram was to be studied outside of the studio together with the manual that accompanied the Buchla synthesizer. Coupled with this assignment was the task of tuning all of the available oscillators to the first six partials of the overtone series. This proved to be especially difficult: the studio's Buchla system was old and the oscillators almost immediately drifted out of tune. It was an excellent lesson because the tuning exercise made us treat the Buchla system as if it were a musical instrument. Also, we were made aware that working with electronic music demanded a refined sense of hearing.

Oliveros demanded an orderliness about our work. Tapes were to be correctly labeled with leaders, and we were to come prepared with our own empty reels, high-quality tape, splicing block, stopwatch, pitch pipe, and good razor. She remarked that it was wise to have your own equipment; that way you could depend upon it.

She also stressed that when you meet the machine (the synthesizer), you meet yourself. In her terms, "You had better walk into the studio with good vibes. If you are disturbed you will most likely make mistakes."

But Oliveros also encouraged us to be creative with the medium, and several of us did improvisatory pieces for our final project. My own piece, Ode to Casper Crooked Tooth (1972), used recorded and modulated dog sounds. The score required that live humanized-dog sounds were to be recorded and also participate in the modulation of the pre-processed material. Class members who wanted to participate were asked to bring pictures of their dogs, which they

were to look at while making the prescribed doglike sounds.
Oliveros was a volunteer for my piece along with seven other
people.   She brought pictures of several of her dogs, and
one fellow actually brought his dog, a large Irish setter.
While we were all sitting in a circle making our canine
sounds, an amazing thing happened: the Irish setter walked
from person to person and silently observed the entire procedure.   This was a performance I will never forget and is
an example of the kind of liberties Oliveros allowed and encouraged in her students. [14]

Notes

1.   From Oliveros's observations about her piece Valentine
(1968) in Elliott Schwartz, Electronic Music (New York:
Praeger, 1973), pp. 246-247.

2.   For more information about the early history of the
San Francisco Tape Music Center see Pauline Oliveros,
"On the Need for Research Facilities for New Music and
Related Arts," Performing Arts Review, IX, 4 (1979),
464-472, and her contribution to "Groups: New Music En-
semble, ONCE Group, Sonic Arts Group, Musica ettronica,"
Source, II, 1 (January 1968), 16.

3.   Oliveros was especially creative in the area of tape delay.   Her article "Tape Delay Techniques for Electronic
Music" was published in The Composer, I, 3 (December
1969), 135-142.

4.   John Rockwell, "The Musical Meditations of Pauline
Oliveros," New York Times, May 25, 1980.   Rockwell
also included Bye Bye Butterfly as one of the fifteen sig-
nificant pieces composed between 1960 and 1969 in his
article "Which Works of the 70's Were Significant," New
York Times, July 27, 1980.   Other music so honored was
Luciano Berio's Sinfonia (1968), Pierre Boulez's Pli Selon
Pli (1957-62), and György Ligeti's Atmospheres (1961).

5.   This information is contained in Hugh Davies, com-
piler, International Electronic Music Catalog (Cambridge:
M. I. T. Press, 1968), p. 21.

6.   Pauline Oliveros, "Some Sound Observations," Source,
January 1968, p. 79.

7. But see Herman Helmholtz's early studies about combination tones in his On the Sensations of Tone (New York:
Dover, 1954), pp. 152-159, 418-429, and 527-536. The
Dover edition is an unabridged and unaltered reprint of the
second (1885) edition of the Ellis translation of Helmholtz's
work. Helmholtz found that sopranos singing together and
certain instruments, such as flutes and reed organs, playing in upper registers often produce combination tones loud
enough to be heard. The accordion is similar in tone production to reed organs and is most susceptible to producing
these combination tones, especially when extra pressure is
applied to the bellows.

8. Oliveros, "Some Sound Observations," p. 79.

9. Oliveros describes her double tape-delay setup in "Tape
Delay Techniques for Electronic Music." Alfred Franken-
stein favorably reviewed I of IV and described it as "a kind
of electronic symphony" in his article "Electronic Music--
Masterpieces and Other Pieces," High Fidelity/Musical
America, XVIII (February 1968), 45.

10. John J. O'Neill, Prodigal Genius: The Life of Nikola
Tesla (New York: Ives Washburn, 1944).

11. In reading the biography of Tesla I found a remarkable
similarity between Cunningham's and Oliveros's artistic activities and Tesla's avant-garde scientific theories and discoveries at the turn of the century.

12. From Oliveros's article about "Canfield" in James
Klosty, editor, Merce Cunningham (New York: Dutton,
1975), pp. 79-80.

13. The successes and failures of the Pavilion project are
described in Billy Klüver, Julie Martin, and Barbara Rose,
editors, Pavilion (New York: Dutton, 1972). Oliveros's
score for A-OK is found on pp. 304-307.

14. Oliveros describes some of her other students' work
in electronic music in her article "Five Scenes" in Numus
West, Spring 1972, p. 36.

5: THEATER PIECES

The period of the mid-1960s to the early 1970s was a time when Oliveros was beginning to analyze the traditions of European performance practice. She noticed how much aura surrounds the composer and performer and how little attention is given to the audience and synthesized her previous musical directions of improvisation and electronic music. Her commitment to continual listening made Oliveros aware of other sensory modalities. She began to write compositions that incorporated theatrical scenarios and often included specific performers, instruments, objects, and meditative practices that had special meaning for her.

Again, the milieu of San Francisco was highly influential with its mime troups, street theater, the Dancers' Workshop, and other experimental groups. It was fortunate that eventually the San Francisco Tape Music Center and the Dancers' Workshop were housed in the same building, because the location gave Oliveros an opportunity to collaborate with and to observe other creative people.

One such occasion took place in 1964, when David Tudor and John Cage visited the Tape Music Center and Oliveros organized a Tudor Fest. Tudor commissioned her to write a piece for him (he is famous for having premiered many of John Cage's keyboard works), so she decided to have Tudor play bandoneon and she would use her accordion. Oliveros designed a score using a mix of improvisational and determinant notation, as in her Outline for Flute, Percussion, and String Bass. She titled the commission Duo for Accordion and Bandoneon (1964).

[68]

As Oliveros and Tudor rehearsed, however, some drastic changes occurred. First, Oliveros kept a mynah bird in her house, where the rehearsals were taking place, and it was always talking while they were playing, so she decided to include the mynah bird as part of the piece. Her ambition to be continually listening began to influence her compositions, and she changed the title to Duo for Accordion and Bandoneon with Possible Mynah Bird Obligato [sic].

Including the bird added a visual dimension, and Oliveros asked Elizabeth Harris to design a stage setup for the Duo. Harris built a beautiful wooden seesaw that moved in the usual up-and-down fashion, but it also had revolving chairs. Harris suspended a bird cage above the seesaw. Amazingly, the seesaw made almost no sound, which was ideal, but Oliveros encountered some serious problems with her piece. It was impossible to read a musical score while seesawing and revolving. The only solution was to abandon the score and create a few simple directions that she and Tudor could memorize. Harris choreographed some motions for the seesaw and Oliveros found that long-held tone clusters from the bandoneon and accordion became fascinating stereophonic sounds as the seesaw moved and turned.

Tudor meticulously prepared Oliveros's piece and the other music he was performing at the Fest. His attention to detail and precision in even the vaguest indeterminate score impressed Oliveros and the other members of the San Francisco Tape Music Center.

Oliveros also collaborated with Ann Halprin, the director of the Dancers' Workshop. She is well known for her extraordinary work in dance. Like Oliveros, Halprin analyzes the relationship between dancers and audience and has synthesized her own concept of what dance should be. She considers all movement to be dance, which is similar to Cage's philosophy of wanting all sound to be music. Halprin's choreography also includes the ritualistic aspects of dance in which performers and audience explore cultural myths in an attempt to erase the dichotomy between art and life.[1]

Oliveros participated in some of these events and wrote The Bath (1966) for Ann Halprin and collaborated with Elizabeth Harris for Seven Passages (1963) and Five for Trumpet and Dancer (1965). Oliveros even collaborated with the San Francisco Mime Troupe, writing

Candelaio (1965), The Exception and the Rule (1965), and The Chronicles of Hell (1965) for them. All of these works were commissioned by R. G. Davis (the founder of the San Francisco Mime Troupe) and performed the year they were composed.

The combined activities of the Dancers' Workshop and the San Francisco Tape Music Center often attracted a large regular audience to their monthly concerts. Some of Oliveros's theater pieces were presented at these concerts, and the pieces that she wrote for the Mime Troupe were performed in the parks and outdoor spaces in the Bay area.

Working with artists outside of music was not unusual; there was an emerging trend to trespass the boundaries of an art form, and many musicians began to include visual elements in their compositions. Cage created a sensation with his Theater Piece (1960), and Stockhausen explored a similar idea in his Originale (1961). Others were experimenting with events called happenings, activities, mixed media, intermedia, and total theater. [2] Although there has been much discussion concerning the similarities and differences among these categories, Oliveros very simply calls her conglomerate compositions "theater pieces," an appropriate title, since she requires lighting, costuming, props, staging, and character portrayal by musicians.

Always sensitive to imagery, Oliveros found that this genre gave her an opportunity to mix humor, emotion, and symbolism in a manner that was both entertaining and serious. But even more important, she found that her penchant for imagery allowed her to make statements about music that were impossible to say in a totally abstract medium, such as symphonies and string quartets or even electronic music, and theater pieces provided the opportunity to use material objects to augment her message. Oliveros's statement was becoming clearer: she wanted the freedom to be herself and to make her own music.

Previously this statement had been focused upon herself as composer, as when she explored the freedom of improvisation and electronic music. Now she experimented with analyzing and exposing what seems to be the shackles of concert music, in which she felt that the performers' musical training discourages the cultivation of musical freedom. Improvisation, so important to Oliveros, is a rare skill for most conservatory- and university-trained musicians.

Also, musicians too frequently recreate the music of the past as sonic museum pieces and ignore the message of live composers.

Pieces of Eight (dedicated to Long John Silver, 1965) is an early example of how Oliveros used visual and sonic imagery as a statement about performance practices. Barney Childs commissioned the piece for the Contemporary Players at the University of Arizona. The score, for an octet of winds, reads like a play. It is easy to imagine a performance, especially as Oliveros describes every detail of costuming, timing, action, props, and even the mental attitude and breathing that should be used during the performance. The title and dedication refer to Robert Louis Stevenson's Treasure Island, and the piece is indeed laden with symbolism and meaning that develop as the drama unfolds and the listener wonders what relationships these have to the music. The stage setup (see page 72) forewarns the audience that this is going to be an unusual performance, and the appearance of musicians dressed in costumes (such as dungarees, tails, pirate outfits, ecclesiastical garb, plumber's attire, and powdered wigs) suggests a bizarre mixture of characters.

The props are visually prominent and crucial to understanding the music. They include a cuckoo clock, eight mechanical alarm clocks, a weather cock, an imposing papier-mâché bust of Beethoven with battery-operated eyes that blink red lights, a wooden packing case, crowbar, cash register, church collection plates, scales, banner, and a large piece of white paper containing an obvious black spot. Each prop produces a sound, such as the mechanical alarm clocks and the wooden packing case, which makes squeaking noises caused by the prying of rusty nails. The composer suggests that the nails be pretreated with rosin to ensure the sonic element. If the objects do not naturally produce sounds, then their appearance in the piece causes a change in the sounds.

Other technological items are: a tape of ticking clocks, telephone, organ, and bird sounds, a short film and a slide of a yellow-headed parrot, and a transparency of a pirate skull and crossbones.

By now the Treasure Island motive is apparent. Recall that the parrot in the story cried "Pieces of Eight, Pieces of Eight" at a crucial time and exposed the presence

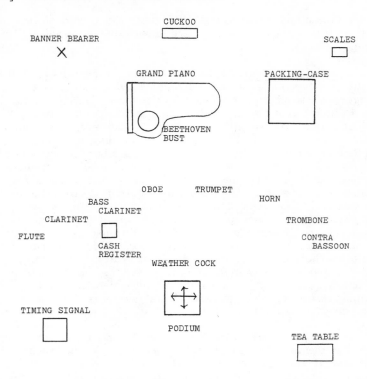

Staging diagram for <u>Pieces of Eight</u>.   Copyright 1980 by Smith Publications.   Used by permission.

of the young Jim Hawkins to the sleeping Long John Silver and his buccaneer comrades.   The skull and crossbones (seen at the end of <u>Pieces of Eight</u>) complete the death motive, which was first introduced when the white paper with the large black spot was passed among several performers during the early part of <u>Pieces of Eight</u>.   (In the story anyone who received the black spot was marked for death.)

The plot of <u>Pieces of Eight</u> is surrealistic and must be described in order to understand how the sounds are used. All enter in procession, except the oboe player, who appears later wearing a fur coat.   The conductor gives the downbeat, but a crowbar is substituted for the customary baton.   The players immediately wind and set their clocks for exactly twelve minutes before 8:00, with the alarms positioned to ring precisely at 8:00. Gradually the instrumentalists make soft and short sounds similar to the ticking clocks, and the conductor begins to open the packing case. The contrabassoonist takes a yellow tape measure and records some measurements of his or her instrument upon a piece of white paper. This is given to the clarinetist, who then transports the document to the conductor--and now the audience sees the black spot.

All continue the ticking and squeaking that imitates the packing-case sounds, but the horn player, who seems out of place in eighteenth-century formal attire, does the following: "... inhale as you stand up slowly. Hold your breath. Bow to your chair. Exhale. Fix your attention on the tea table; inhale, hold your breath, walk slowly to the tea table, bow to the table, and exhale. Breathe normally and start the tea water heating."3

Oliveros has similar kinds of instructions for all the performers. Players are to be serious and movements must be made slowly and thoughtfully. Although some of the sections in Pieces of Eight are humorous, the musicians maintain their characterization simply by paying attention to what they are doing.

The most dramatic part is the entrance of the furry oboist, a clownlike figure who runs through the hall and then slowly takes his seat among the octet and begins to play a fast and furious etude. This abruptly ends and the oboist runs a course around the perimeter of the stage, stopping at the scales to be weighed and then performing calisthenics before exiting. All of this activity must be accomplished in two minutes.

Meanwhile the flutist and the trumpeter march around the center of the stage tracing a figure-eight pattern while playing melodic major seconds in march tempo, their sounds coordinated with those of the continuously ticking clocks. Other actions include gathering around the piano with heads close together and yelling "hey!" and the unison ringing of all the alarm clocks at 8:00.

This event causes a change in imagery. The musicians perform eight measures of organ-grinder music, but the special feature is the cash register, which is sounded as the penultimate measure and the trigger for the bulb eyes of the Beethoven bust to blink on and off. The organ-grinder music is replaced by taped organ music, and an offertory procession is begun, collectors being careful to jangle the metal plates as audience members contribute.   Other visual and sonic images begin to accumulate quickly.   The organ music is enhanced by bird calls and a screeching parrot as the slide of a parrot and the projected image of a pirate skull and crossbones ends the piece.

Obviously, money and the number eight are the themes of Pieces of Eight, but their significance is more than mere entertainment.   The themes provide the structure.   Eight is reflected in several aspects: the instrumentation is a wind octet; the clocks are set to ring at eight (the audience can see the cuckoo clock so they are aware of the time); there are eight cues that divide the total duration of sixteen minutes into eight two-minute sections; the flute player and trumpet player trace a figure-eight pattern as they march in the center of the stage; the organ-grinder music is eight measures long; and the oboe player sits down at exactly the eighth minute.

The money theme is developed, too.   There are several money containers: the packing case enclosing a supposed buried treasure, the cash register, and the collection plates.   The money motive is also clothed with ritualistic meanings.   The audience is asked to give some of their monies, and the organ-grinder music imitates sounds associated with performing for money.   These sounds suddenly change into church organ music to accompany the formal offertory procession through the audience.   The plates are then taken to the piano, which becomes an altar--a sinister one, as the image of a skull and crossbones gradually emerges behind it.   Also, the offertory is headed by the bust of Beethoven, whose blinking eyes reflect his interest in this monetary situation.

The bust of Beethoven is one of several "head" motives.   The film of a yellow-headed parrot led the first procession through the audience and the projected skull and crossbones is the final gesture of the piece.   All of the performers had their heads together when they shouted "hey" into the piano.

Many sonic and visual measuring devices are present, such as the ticking clocks, tape measure, weather cock, cuckoo clock, weighing scale, and cash register.   All of these add tension to the piece, as one wonders what is being measured; why are the clocks ticking, and what is the meaning of the "black spot"?

It is the audience that has been marked with the "black spot": the members of the audience are being robbed of their money, and Oliveros, as composer, has been playing the part of Long John Silver in looking for the treasure buried in their pockets. The first page of the score reminds the performers that "all monies collected must be sent directly to the composer." When asked why she wrote the piece Oliveros answered: "I really needed money!"4

Pieces of Eight marked a dramatic change in Oliveros's style. There is no improvisation so as to keep the performers in character. Instead, the audience is continually improvising different interpretations for what is happening. Although Pieces of Eight does include a tape, the live sounds seem to be electroniclike material that one could expect to hear in musique-concrète, an early category of electronic music that used such nonmusical sounds as ticking clocks, squeaking nails, and noisy cash registers. Oliveros wanted her audience to realize why she used the sounds she chose and how her composition was organized. That is why she required that the musicians be sonic actors and assume a body language and appearance that visually reinforced the sounds themselves.

Oliveros's sense of humor is evident in Pieces of Eight, but underlying this humor is the message of death to concert music, flashy etudes, and symphonic maestros. Some of the critics of a San Francisco performance missed the whole point. Probably they were trying to interpret the composition solely as music and ignored the symbolic theatrical elements. The joke was on them especially if they contributed to the collection. However, Dean Wallace, a critic, writing for the San Francisco Chronicle, called Oliveros "a master at translating the ideas of the theater-of-the-absurd into a quasi-musical situation."5

In addition to character portrayal Pieces of Eight exhibits Oliveros's interest in experimenting with the act of performing. She says, "Musicians' actions as performers and the visual elements are as important as the sounds produced. My concern with stage behavior and its unusual nature tends to disorient audiences and is intended to disorient the performer and break stereotyped approaches to performance, at the same time there is a desire for the individual

personality to come through and take a vital role in the music ... unarticulated elements which have become part of
the background in traditional music are part of the foreground
in my theater pieces."6   The musicians are not anonymous
figures in concert attire who formally sit in prescribed
places.   The conductor is more interested in looking for
money than leading the musicians, and the horn player really wants time off for tea.   The oboist is the star because it
appears that this musician is free to do whatever he or she
wants.   Actually the only music that the oboist plays is the
chosen etude.

Oliveros was experimenting with stage behavior, but
the real significance of Pieces of Eight is her emerging
interest in the audience's reaction.   Later her compositions
would incorporate more audience participation, but with
Pieces of Eight Oliveros's attention is turning away from
being totally preoccupied with the act of composition to a
concern for the audience and how they will hear, understand, and possibly participate in her piece.

Shortly after joining the faculty at the University of
California, San Diego, Oliveros composed Double Basses at
Twenty Paces (1968) for Bertram Turetzky and Allan Gold-
man.   The piece is about the personalities of these men and
the idiosyncrasies of bass players in general.   Turetzky was
a faculty member with Oliveros and is a leader in promoting
new works for the double bass (he commissioned the Outline
for Flute, Percussion, and String Bass and premiered it at
Yale University).   Although Double Basses at Twenty Paces
is a musical portrait of him, it can be performed by any
two bassists who have a theatrical flair and strong fingers.

Oliveros designed the piece to feature many of the
trademarks of double-bass players.   They follow the ordinary procedures of tuning and matching pitches, but then they
must match complex timbres as each player challenges the
other to produce unusual sounds on the instrument.   They
discuss the qualities and disadvantages of the German and
French bows, tell why they like their particular bass, play
segments of Dragonetti etudes (literature that is part of
every bassist's training) and sections of familiar songs, play
pizzicati passages, and even slap and twirl their instruments
several times, something Oliveros remembers from her days
of playing in Texas bands.

The action is a parody of a fencing match.   Mauricio

Kagel also composed a theater piece using a duel that he titled Match (1964). Oliveros says she was not aware of Kagel's work until later. In Oliveros's piece program notes inform the audience about the aggressive and competitive spirit needed for the sport and describe the basic attacks. Her piece is a highly textured montage. There are a referee (conductor), two seconds (stage managers), a box of bows, and the two contestants (bassists). The seconds place the music, stands, and stools on a spot that is ten paces each from the center, and the bassists select their bows, gesture in the formal manner of fencing, and begin. The referee cues sections and silently conducts specified passages from Beethoven's Fifth Symphony in C minor (1807), the most obvious being the highly motivic first movement. The bassists play quotations from this symphony (all authentic bass passages, such as the opening theme of the third movement), but they are not always playing the passages that the referee is conducting; the sounding music noticeably differs in meter and tempo from the visual conducted patterns. Other superimpositions occur: two Dragonetti etudes, one slow and the other fast, are performed simultaneously, and "Stardust," in D♭, and "Sweet Georgia Brown," in G, are played together. Their bitonal relationship is important: the G being the dominant of the C minor symphony, which the audience soon recognizes as the theme or tonic of Double Basses, and the D♭ is the Neapolitan of C. Later visual actions confirm the structural and decorative significances of these pitch areas.

There are several improvised sections, but these are highly controlled. A sample instruction reads, "Interpret the following question as a phrase on your bass, addressed to your opponent: 'Can you squawk like a chicken?'"7 Two other questions, asking about grunting like a pig or braying like a jackass, follow. The opponent answers twice with the theme from the Symphony's third movement, then twirls the bass and plays a modulation to the D♭ (the Neapolitan) as if the tonal relation has been spun around.

The climax occurs when both performers begin an inaudible pizzicato tremolo (a difficult performance technique on the bass) on the G dominant. The tremolo must get louder, and, if necessary, the player may add his or her voice to increase the volume. The loser is the first person who quits.

There really is no loser, however, because suddenly

the lights go off; a tape of crashing thunder resolves into
the final coda of the Fifth Symphony; and a projected slide
of Beethoven's death mask slowly comes into focus.   This
cadence, like the one in Pieces of Eight, is a sudden change
in emotional tone from humorous to serious.   Although the
audience realizes that Oliveros has been poking fun at the
competitive spirit that exists among performers, the Beethoven symbolism is mysterious, especially since the death
mask is a grimace.   Other composers, such as George
Rochberg and Stockhausen, have quoted Beethoven, but Oliveros's references are strange.   Is she mocking the classics or perhaps presenting Beethoven "dressed up" as Oliveros?   A series of postcards sent to friends depicting her
as Beethoven (the resemblance was amazing) may confirm
the latter.   In an interview conducted by Moria Roth, however, Oliveros discussed how much she has always liked
Beethoven's music. [8]   As a child she was impressed by the
picture of Beethoven that hung in her grandmother's piano
studio.

Oliveros was even more bizarre with Aeolian Partitions (1969), a piece commissioned by the Aeolian Players
at Bowdoin College and published by the Bowdoin College
Music Press.   Not knowing the players personally, she
asked for a picture of the group before beginning to compose the piece and tried to imagine the personality of each
member.

Aeolian Partitions requires a proscenium stage,
lighting, props, and costuming.   The instrumentation is for
flute, clarinet, violin, cello, and piano, and all performers
are required to wear formal dress.   A page turner and two
extras (who are especially familiar to the audience) are
needed to complete the action of the piece.   The following
props are used: a broom, newspaper, flashlight with red
blinker and white beam, gong on a stand, bow, suction-cup
arrows, and quiver.   The stage crew must have seven six-
volt flasher lamps of amber color and equipment to project
a slide of the Star of David.

The piece is a statement about duality, a partitioning
into parts.   The musicians both act and perform on their
instruments, but the acting is a transformation of a normal
performance gesture.   For example, the pianist lifts his or
her hands above the keyboard in preparation for a loud
crashing chord but instead stretches and yawns as if bored.
Later the performer reaches inside the piano to play a

pizzicato string but pulls out a newspaper from inside the
instrument and leisurely reads.

Each instrumentalist plays a familiar cadenza from
concert literature but abruptly stops before the resolution of
the cadenza, and the cellist immediately appears with a
broom (a transformation of the cello) and begins to sweep,
as if to clean up the music of those cadenzas. Later the
cello case is transformed into a coffin and is carried off
the stage by pallbearer performers accompanied by piccolo
"wake music."

The violin is transformed into a bow and arrow tip-
ped with suction cups. The violinist shoots an arrow at a
large gong, which is then removed as if the resonating gong
were in its last stages of life.

A radio becomes a musical instrument and has its
solo cadenza as one of the extras (the composer suggests
that the Dean of the school perform this part) walks across
the stage while carrying the radio.

Lights, too, have an instrumental function. There is
a total blackout after the radio cadenza and during the following violin cadenza. The pianist, flashlight in hand,
searches for the sounds and illuminates the violinist from
feet to head and then directs the light toward the audience.

The presence of a drone on A^5 establishes a unity
throughout the first part of Aeolian Partitions. Much of the
drone is provided by the flutist and clarinetist, who move
about the stage and audience areas while sounding A's. Each
moment of the drone is carefully shaped, as shown in Example 15. Every performer at some point plays the drone as
if to color the pitch with his or her personality. The violinist performs the pitch espressivo with an extremely wide
vibrato and in one bow; the pianist plays the lowest A sfor-
zando and with the sustaining pedal depressed; while at the
downbeat of the piece the cellist soundlessly draws the bow
across the D string while fingering the A. Even the piccolo's
"wake music" is centered around A.

Just as the sounds are transformed into gestures and
the radio and lights become instruments, so the content of
Aeolian Partitions becomes transformed and divides into two
distinct formal sections that at first seem totally unrelated.
After the funeral procession where the cello case is carried

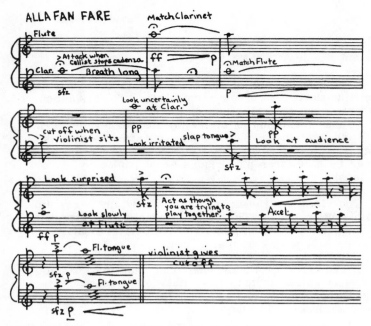

Example 15. Drone "alla fan fare" in <u>Aeolian Partitions</u>. Copyright 1970 by Bowdoin College Press. Used by permission.

```
x = volt flasher lamps
```

 = chair

PROJECTION SURFACE FOR STAR OF DAVID*

VIOLA
X

ALTO FLUTE
X

PIANO

X

X   X

BASS CLARINET
X

CELLO
X

* A slide screen should not be used. The Star of David should appear on the back wall above the players, even if the wall or backdrop is not very reflective.

Flasher positions for "telepathic improvisation." Copyright 1970 by Bowdoin College Press. Used by permission.

off the stage, the lights dim and finally go out while seven
amber flasher lights are placed as in the diagram on page 80.

The players reenter, take their place, and begin a
telepathic improvisation. The directions are:

> Each performer concentrates on another single per-
> former. When he hears an interval or chord men-
> tally, he plays one of the pitches and assumes that
> he is sending the other pitch or pitches to the other
> performer by mental telepathy. Each performer
> plays only long tones, but varies dynamics, vi-
> brato, and timbre. He tries to influence different
> performers and to make silences by becoming
> mentally blank.... The audience may be invited
> to join in the telepathic improvisation with the
> following instructions:

> Concentrate on a single performer. Try to
> hear a pitch mentally. See if you can influence the
> performer to play your pitch by mental telepathy.
> If you cannot hear a pitch mentally try to influence
> the performer to play higher or lower, louder or
> softer or to be silent. 9

After ten minutes a slide of the Star of David is projected on the rear wall of the stage and the performers
gradually substitute vocal sounds for their instrumental ones.
They prepare to end the improvisation and slowly exit while
carrying the flasher lamps.

The telepathic improvisation is a clam meditative action that is just the opposite of the furious cadenzas heard
previously. Originally cadenzas were meant to be improvisations in which performers were allowed to engage in creative activity of their own, but this tradition has all but dis-
appeared as performers play standard written-out cadenzas.
Thus, while Oliveros transforms the cadenzas into a true
improvisation, she also explores a complementary performance mode, one in which communication takes place without
the use of words or score but through concentration based
upon the power of mental suggestion shared among the performers and the audience. The concentration and communication become an actuality when one mentally hears sounds
and then reproduces them. Again, this is just the opposite
of the first part of Aeolian Partitions, in which performers
prepare to make sounds that instead become gestures.

The composer Elliott Schwartz, who was the light
technician for the Bowdoin premiere, has remarked that
Oliveros's theater pieces have a dualistic nature.   They
begin with a light and humorous feeling and then change to
a serious and sometimes mystical or even menacing mood
for the end, as in Pieces of Eight and Double Basses at
Twenty Paces. 10   He associated these mood changes with
the changes in lighting, but the duality is even more strongly controlled by the imagery that shapes the composition.
In this piece the encircled Star of David, which is pictured
on the cover of the score, determines every structural element.

At first the Star of David seems to be unrelated to
any of the activities or props used in Aeolian Partitions.
Usually the hexagram is associated with Israel's Magen
David, the shield of David.   The symbol is also an alche-
mistic talisman representing the transmutation of fire and
water.   But, though Oliveros has always been interested in
the Tarot (she frequently does readings for her friends) and
used Tarot symbolism in The Wheel of Fortune, she did not
realize the hexagram's talismanic function.   She intended the
figure to be interpreted as a Jewish emblem, but it is curious that the Tarot interpretation is an accurate primary
image of Aeolian Partitions, just as money and eight were
images that dominated Pieces of Eight.   The hexagram explains the many transmutations that occur throughout the
piece: sounds become gestures; objects become instruments;
the Dean of the school becomes a musician; unresolved cadenzas become telepathic improvisations; lights become the
hexagram (as explained in the next paragraph); and finally
the audience is given the opportunity to control sound with
telepathic power.   It would seem that the Tarot was unconsciously dominating Oliveros's compositional decisions in its
own form of telepathy.

The hexagram is seen in all of the stage action,
which traces out triangular patterns, often creating two triangles that touch or overlap, as in the hexagram.   The
opening gesture of the piece places the violinist and cellist
together in the center of the stage while the flutist and
clarinetist are positioned in the right and left back corners
of the auditorium.   The audience is encased in a magic tri-
angle of sound.

Even more mysterious is the way the lighting reveals
the hexagram.   The piece begins with a red spotlight shining

on an empty chair. The light fades when the players enter, but later another red light appears as the blinker of the pianist's flashlight, and finally seven amber flashlights form the setup for the telepathic improvisation. The placement of these lights creates an elongated representation of the hexagram with the points of the triangles being marked by amber lights blinking in the darkness. See the figure on the bottom of page 80. The final illumination is the projection of the Star of David. If the audience does not recognize the importance of the hexagram, then the image is such a powerful archetypal symbol that it affects a person at other levels of consciousness.

Having experimented with the telepathic improvisation, Oliveros's interest in theater changed in the early 1970s as she began to develop meditative techniques. Her theater pieces became materially simpler while at the same time increasing in philosophical complexities.

It is not surprising that the title of her next theater piece is Link (1971), an environmental work for specialized and nonspecialized performers. It was commissioned by Larry Livingston. In 1976 Oliveros submitted Link, retitled Bonn Feier, to a contest sponsored by the city of Bonn, Germany, for music to be performed in outdoor spaces. She won the contest, and the piece was performed as part of the city's 1977 Beethoven Festival--which was curious considering her use of Beethoven imagery in previous pieces. Link, however, makes no reference to Beethoven. (I shall be referring to the composition as Link rather than Bonn Feier because the former title is so symbolic of the piece.)

Link is intended to be performed in a college or university environment. The campus becomes a theater where everyone, knowingly or not, is a performer. Oliveros designed the composition with the intention that "Link is to gradually and subtly sub-vert perception so that normal activity seems as strange or displaced as any of the special activities."[11] This change in perception is accomplished by juxtaposing abnormal sights, sounds, activities, and movements with their normal counterparts.

Performers prepare for the piece by making a sound map of the campus, notating continuous, intermittent, and probable sounds that normally occur. These sounds constitute the campus's sonic drone and, together with sounds that

are judged to be the most unusual, are designated sound
marks and indicated on the sound map.

The normal dronelike sounds become abnormal in
several ways.   First, costumed guardians are posted near
the sound marks and silently point to the sound source.
Second, musicians, who are also positioned at the sound
marks, reinforce the environmental sounds by playing
pitches, dynamics, and so forth that blend with the sound
mark.

Normal sounds associated with campus activities are
also part of Link.   Lecturing and conversing become the
sonic material of mummers, jesters, or actors.   These
clownlike figures are costumed as specific characters and
move about the campus trying to engage people in ridiculous
conversations.   Foreign faculty members and students are
encouraged to speak their native languages during the times
that Link is being performed.

Even instruments talk.   Drummers are to devise a
language using two drum tones to imitate English words and
phrases.   The drummers send messages to each other via
their drum language.   Natural sound makers converse.   One
special group of performers moves about the campus using
whistles and other objects to make intermittent sound signals that are within the hearing range of at least one other
performer.

The theme of total theater juxtaposed upon campus
activity is also developed by nonspecialized performers,
such as faculty and staff, who are invited to perform their
normal duties abnormally.   For instance, Oliveros suggests
that a physical-plant worker might wear a tuxedo or people
in the surrounding community could perform their normal
duties in an abnormal campus setting, such as a farmer
milking a cow in the campus parking lot.   She also recom-
mends that normal performance groups function in unusual
ways, such as having performances unannounced or in
strange places.

Link is choreographed.   Dancers, athletes, and non-
specialists explore the campus with extremely slow and
repetitious gestures.   Even a march takes place as picket-
ers slowly and silently walk inch by inch carrying blank
signs.   The grand finale is a ritualistic circle ceremony
where all the performers gradually come together and chant

the word "link" continuously and simultaneously while building an accelerando. This final cadence should take at least
an hour to occur.

The minimum time span for Link is fifteen hours,
but Oliveros suggests that the piece could be extended over
periods of weeks, months, or a year. Her score is designed to encourage participation on all levels from the highly specialized performer to the person who wants to participate in a minimal fashion. Not everyone needs to perform
all of the time.

Once again Oliveros tried to guarantee that the piece
will work by carefully specifying performer attitude. She
says, "It's [Link's] success depends on the full commitment,
attentiveness and understanding of the knowing performers.
Each performer must be willing to undertake his or her part
with the understanding that devoted and UNDIVIDED attention
to the chosen tasks, no matter how long they are, is necessary."[12]

Like her other theater pieces, Link combines fun and
seriousness. The ending reveals the meaning and the image
of the link, which structures what might appear to be ridiculous and unrelated events into a unified whole. The bonn
feier or celebration image used in the German performance
also works as the structure of the piece, because the events
do not take place in a college setting but rather in a city
where the entire community has an opportunity to participate.
The cadence for this performance was a bonfire.[13] Abnormal perceptions produce dissonances that are only resolved
when everyone recognizes that all of these activities are in-
tentionally linked together.

The ultimate realization would be that Link is a series
of tunings. Like Pieces of Eight and Aeolian Partitions, the
performers are told how to tune their attention and awareness: total concentration must be focused upon the chosen
tasks. The observation of the campus's sonic drone shows
a person how much of the sonic environment is tuned out,
and that the content of daily consciousness is self-constructed
in terms of normal expectations.

Notes

1. Activities of the Dancers' Workshop are documented in

Lawrence Halprin, The RSVP Cycles: Creative Processes in the Human Environment (New York: Braziller, 1969).

2.   For more information about developments in theater see E. T. Kirby, Total Theatre (New York: Dutton, 1969); Michael Kirby, Art of Time: Essays on the Avant-Garde (New York: Dutton, 1969); and David Cope, New Directions in Music, 2nd ed., (Dubuque, Iowa: Brown, 1971), pp. 115-145.

3.   Pieces of Eight, page 14 of the manuscript copy.   Reprinted by permission of the publisher.

4.   Oliveros collected $75 from two San Francisco performances and considers this sum a more generous amount than if she were paid royalties for the piece.

5.   Dean Wallace, San Francisco Chronicle, May 4, 1965.

6.   Pauline Oliveros, "Career Narrative."   This document is the vita submitted to the Guggenheim Foundation.

7.   Pauline Oliveros, Double Basses at Twenty Paces, page 8 of the manuscript copy.   Reprinted by permission of the publisher.

8.   Moria Roth, "An Interview with Pauline Oliveros," New Performance, I, 2 (1977), 41-51.

9.   Oliveros, Aeolian Partitions, page 5.   Reprinted by permission of the publisher.

10.   Elliott Schwartz, "Some Thoughts on Pauline Oliveros," footnote 10 in Oliveros's "Career Narrative."

11.   Pauline Oliveros, Link, published in Women's Work, a collection of performance scores.   It can be obtained by writing to Anna Lockwood, Music Department, Hunter College, CUNY, 695 Park Avenue, New York, NY 10021.   The score is also available as Bonn Feier from Smith Publications.

12.   Oliveros, Link, unp.   Reprinted by permission of the publisher.

13.   For a discussion of the Bonn performance see Roth, "An Interview with Pauline Oliveros."

6: CONSCIOUSNESS STUDIES

Oliveros's theater pieces were a prelude to a new dimension in her work. By the early 1970s she began to study consciousness seriously. Her natural affinity for imagery and the intuitive process of improvisation eventually led her to investigate T'ai Chi, karate, ritual, dreams, ceremonies, mandalas, and the latest research about meditation. As a result her work assumed a new dimension and a direction that some people might not even consider to be music.

Several events influenced this change. The hostile spirit of the times expressed through student riots, the Vietnam War, and the rise of the women's movement caused Oliveros to turn inward in an effort to discover what was the meaning of these energies and how they affected her. No longer could she compose with the kind of humor she had shown in Pieces of Eight or Double Basses at Twenty Paces.

One solution was to return to her accordion and spend time vocally droning with it and listening to the results. She began to notice changes in the sound and in herself. Droning was calming. Others were interested in similar kinds of activities. Oliveros met Al Huang, who at that time was teaching a dance class at Long Beach City State College and also T'ai Chi sessions at Rancho Santa Fe, not far from where Oliveros lived. Her interest in long drones resembled T'ai Chi's slowly moving body patterns, so she improvised for some of the classes, translating T'ai Chi's synchronization of breath and movement to her accordion playing.

[87]

Since others wanted to join her improvisation sessions, Oliveros formed the ♀ Ensemble, a group of ten women who met weekly to work with long tones. She tried various ways of guiding and shaping these improvisations and slowly began to realize that she was working with new and exciting compositional material. The results of this experience and research about consciousness and meditation culminated in her Sonic Meditations and other related compositions.

Huang's work with T'ai Chi interested Oliveros, and she began to consider studying a formal body language. She chose karate. Her karate teacher, Lester Ingber, is a theoretical physicist who also studies consciousness. Together they spent many hours discussing models of consciousness and how these were operating in karate, music, and other meditative disciplines. [1]

The karate began to effect some changes in her life, and Oliveros wanted to understand what was happening to her personally. She investigated psychology, especially the work of Carl Jung, and this led her to the study of myth and ritual. She bought many of Joseph Campbell's books, like The Masks of God, [2] Mircea Eliade's studies of world religions, [3] Jerome Rothenberg's Technicians of the Sacred, [4] and later Robert Ornstein's works about human consciousness. Her own interest in personal imagery caused Oliveros to investigate the latest research about dreaming.

It was not unusual for Oliveros to consider these interests as part of her professional research. The Music Department of the University of California at San Diego encouraged faculty and students to study areas that might at first seem to have little or no relation to music. Several faculty members were learning about the two hemispheres of the brain. Frequently departmental seminars (rather faithfully attended by faculty and students) featured lectures given by people outside the field of music, such as Joseph Bogen, who presented neurophysiological research concerning split brain patients, veterans who had injuries requiring lobectomies. [5] The Medical School and the Music Department collaborated on projects relating to understanding the physiology of contemporary vocal techniques and Robert Erickson was working with Diana Deutsch of the Psychology Department in performing experiments related to hearing. [6] At the same time Roger Reynolds was writing his book Mind Models, [7] and all of the faculty were joining efforts to locate funding for an independent research center for new music so they could further explore these areas. The Music Department did receive several important grants from the Rockefeller and Ford Foundations, and the Center for Music Experiment is now a leader in the area of computer music. 8

One of the immediate outcomes of her personal research was that Oliveros became interested in dream and sonic imagery. As preliminary study she attended several seminars taught by Ron Lane, a psychologist at the University. He lectured about the nature of consciousness, stressing that the content of dreams was a personal language and that dreams should be used in a positive way. Students in the course were required to keep a dream journal as a technique for intensifying their personal awareness. 9

This was an exercise that Oliveros had already begun for herself. She used the dream journal as a way of improving her compositional skills. She would write down her dream from beginning to end without any hesitation or editing, just as she performed I of IV or Bye Bye Butterfly in real time. She was interested in the clarity of the language, the flow of thought, and the power inherent in the imagery. She claims that she did not really learn how to write until she was thirty-one and began to record her dreams. She discussed her dreams often and even published some of them in Numus West, a short-lived journal dedicated to the cause of new music, which featured four articles by Oliveros. The following dream is from her article titled "Divisions Underground": "Once I dreamed I was on the bottom of the ocean twanging the bones of an old sea captain who had gone down with his treasure. I reached past his blue coat and brass buttons and sounded the depths, vengefully playing on his ribs like a Siren, tempting fate with my human guitar. I doubt that I am too reverent. "10

It was at this same time that she began to realize that her work was moving in the direction of oral tradition. Her compositions, especially the theater pieces, were not in traditional notation but rather recipes that told people what to do. Because her scores are prose compositions, they can be misinterpreted since words are often ambiguous, and that is why Oliveros likes to be present for a performance.

In addition to her dream journal Oliveros also kept a sound journal as another way of practicing her composi-

tional and attentional skills. She had been noticing environmental sounds for a long time, and instead of using a tape
recorder to document them she began to capture these in
her notebook, describing both the physical property of the
sounds and how they affected her. She published some of
this material in Numus West. The following is her description of an environmental sound that she heard on campus:

> From a Sound Journal 10-18-71 UCSD
> Leitmotiv
> It took a while to learn to look ahead of
> the actual sound in order to see the jet or jets.
> I look up only because I know the source is up;
> otherwise, the location would be obscure. It
> comes to consciousness first with a high-pitched
> whine which cycles through the partials of the en-
> gine drone. While droning inexorably, the sound
> is reverberant, reflected from many places in the
> landscape. As the pressure wave passes through
> the campus, it peaks when the lowest part of the
> sound seems to sweep or drag across the ground.
> There are usually many responses from the wooden-
> frame building. A window rattles in sympathy, an
> on-going lecture or concert is always masked by
> the sound, sometimes every 5 or 6 minutes. My
> sternum vibrates, too. With really close jets the
> sound usually distorts at some point, like an over-
> driven speaker. I suppose this is actually the dis-
> tortion of my own over-driven ear. Sometimes
> the jet sounds pop into hearing suddenly without
> any gradual crescendo from the threshold of audi-
> bility. Depending upon my state of mind, I can
> love it or leave it ... but a volume control would
> be nice. The only way for a composer to beat it
> is to include it. Try Nine and a Half for Henry
> (and Wilbur and Orville) by Robert Erickson. 11

   Simultaneously with the dream seminars and her work
with the ♀ Ensemble, Oliveros was learning about focusing
attention and awareness in karate movements. She began to
apply some of these principles to her work with listening.
She wondered about being able to defocus the ears and how
music can be listened to as a whole. Was it possible for
time to become space?12

   She continued her research about human consciousness and found the work of Robert Ornstein, a psychologist

at the Langley Porter Institute in San Francisco (who lectured several times in the San Diego area), helpful. Ornstein promoted the scientific study of meditation, parapsychology, and intuition. He stressed that consciousness was selective and that we only register the necessary sensory internal inputs. In his words "we choose our consciousness at each moment."13

Ornstein was emphatic about the necessity of Western culture to begin to train the intuitive mode, a real concern for Oliveros, especially in her improvisation and teaching. In his later book The Mind Field Ornstein made the following statement: "I propose, then, two complementary principles in human mentation: an ordered sequencer which underlies language and 'rational' mentation, and a simultaneous processor employed for coordination of movement in space, for artistic creativity and reception, for the tonal aspect of music...."14 Ornstein included intuition as part of the simultaneous processor.

However, Lester Ingber, Oliveros's karate instructor, was the most important influence upon her work. In 1968 he completed a scientific study of the physical principles operative in karate. He later expanded his work to analysis of how attentional dynamics function in other instructional methodologies and was trying to create a model of consciousness that incorporated analytical and intuitive thought processes. During the many years that he taught physics and karate Ingber observed that often students fail to achieve the correct solution to a problem because they limit their analyses to a narrow range of possibilities and neglect to incorporate information from their breadth of attention. Ingber describes this area of thought as a diffused processing of patterned information that is often intuitive. Together with a part-time staff at an alternative junior-senior high school in Solana Beach, California, Ingber taught courses that developed and trained both depth and breadth of attention in the sciences and the arts. In 1979 he helped Oliveros design a holistic analysis course that she taught to performers, composers, critics, and visual artists at the University of California at San Diego.

Shortly after beginning karate lessons with Ingber, Oliveros conducted her own experimental and artistic study of meditation. During the winter quarter of 1973 she had a faculty fellowship in the Project for Music Experiment, an early name for the Center for Music Experiment. Twenty

people participated in the study and agreed to observe the
following rules, which Oliveros stated in her first memorandum (January 15, 1973) to the participants:

1. Commitment--regular attendance from 3 PM
    to 5 PM Mon.-Fri. (Except for emergencies
    beyond control.)

2. Silence--On entering the space become non-
    verbal except when an instructor requests
    verbal feedback.   Remain non-verbal until you
    leave the space.   Do not share information or
    talk about the project in any way, no matter
    how trivial, to anyone at all until the project
    is over. (Exception: Dr. Lane is available
    by appointment ... if there is something you
    can not hold.)

3. Diary--Include everything! Feelings, ideas,
    observations, fantasies, dreams, images,
    casual commentary, description, attitudes,
    reactions concerning the training sessions,
    and the project as a whole. Feedback to the
    group will be requested from time to time.

4. No Smoking--Please do not smoke during any
    training session.

Questions for your consideration: Do these rules
serve you? How? Do they hinder you? How?
What effects do you notice? When are they irri-
tants? When are they helpful? Can you keep
them?[15]

This specificity about rules and the seriousness of
commitments has always been typical of Oliveros's work.
She considers it notational precision.   Not all of the participants were musicians, although there were some graduate music students enrolled.   Oliveros also enlisted the
help of Ron Lane from the Psychology Department, Reginald
Bickford (who had studied brain research) from the Medical
School, and Bruce Rittenbach, a graduate student in the Music Department who was in charge of the electronic equipment.   Individual biofeedback and electroencephalogram sessions were arranged for each participant.

The project was not successful, probably because
there were too many variables to make conclusions, but the
research was an impetus for Oliveros to compose Meditations XII to XXV and premiere Phantom Fathom (1973), a
theater piece using sonic meditations and rituals.[16]

After the fellowship Oliveros wrote an article, "On Sonic Meditation," published in the Painted Bride Quarterly, in which she formulated exactly what she meant by meditation, attention, and awareness. She described meditation as simply dwelling upon an object and distinguished her use of the term as secular meditation as opposed to meditation used for religious reasons. Attention and awareness are difficult terms and to my knowledge have not been precisely defined or even adequately described in psychology. In 1980 Oliveros deleted the term awareness and substituted global and focal attention as descriptions of what Ingber termed breadth and depth of attention. In 1974, however, she had cautiously written: "Attention seems to be equated with mental activity and to be aroused by interest or desire. Awareness seems to be equated with the body's sensory receptivity. It is activated, or present, during pleasure or pain. Either attention or awareness can interfere with the other depending on the intensity of interest or the intensity of stimulation. When either attention or awareness predominates or gets out of balance, the other tends to drift or becomes unconscious...."17

She described how to tune attention and awareness, much as if these functions of consciousness were potentiometers on an oscillator. "Attention is narrow, pointed, and selective. Awareness is broad, diffuse, and inclusive. Both have a tunable range: attention can be honed to a finer and finer point. Awareness can be expanded until it seems all inclusive."18

Oliveros was also concerned about training and tuning attention in an educational context, and in the spring of 1975 she submitted a proposal for an internal grant from UC/San Diego that would permit her to study attentional modes in teaching basic musicianship. She did not receive the grant, but the following section from that proposal shows how she understood the functions of attention and awareness in a musical situation:

> The skill of a musician depends on the synthesis of aural, visual, and somatic attention and awareness. He or she must be able to hear mentally as well as physically, see and interpret musical symbols and cues, respond correctly as a singer, conductor or instrumentalist. Attention and awareness may be tuned outward toward the environment or inward to the imagination and memory. Aural and somatic attention can be turned outward while visual

attention is turned inward or any combination of
these modes of attention and awareness might be
in effect.   An individual whose attention and awareness is turned entirely inward might be considered
to be out of touch with reality.   An individual whose
attention and awareness is turned entirely outward
might be considered to be out of touch with himself.   What is necessary for growth and development for the whole person is the ability to focus
attention and find awareness in each area, inward
or outward, flexibly, or at will in any combination
of the modes.   The separation of attention and
awareness is a useful concept. [19]

In addition to being able to separate and tune these
two modes Oliveros wanted to effect changes in consciousness.   She studied Carl Jung's model of consciousness,
which included the collective and personal consciousnesses,
and was fascinated how readily accessible are the material
from these two levels plus the collective unconsciousness
during dreams and fantasy states.

Oliveros was particularly sensitive to the mandala,
a circular image used as a meditation object in Tibetan
Buddhism and other religions and societies.   Jung discovered and studied mandalas as a visual form in his own
dreams and those of his patients.   He considered the mandalas as cryptograms of his whole being actively at work.
The circle represented harmony and integration, and the
shapes within it were dynamic symbols that were paths to
the deep levels of his inner self. [20]

Although the main shape of a mandala is a circle,
the interior can be arranged in different ways.   Often it is
a series of concentric forms and sometimes it is divided
into quadrants, a shape Jung called a "psychological view
finder" and one that Oliveros frequently uses.   As a meditation object the mandala's center is supposed to attract the
attention and be a special source of spiritual power, a point
where attention and awareness come to perfect balance.

Mandalas are not exclusively an Eastern form but
have been used as a therapeutic tool in Indian sandpainting.
Some art critics interpret the circle as a logo of feminine
consciousness, and Jung considered it to be the preeminent
symbol for our own time in his essay "Flying Saucers: A
Modern Myth. "[21]

Oliveros had used several mandala forms in her theater pieces: The Wheel of Fortune, the clock in Pieces of Eight, and the circled Star of David in Aeolian Partitions. It is even possible to consider the sonic web in "Spider Song" and the principle of tape delay as circular forms. The logo ♀ of the ♀ Ensemble is a mandala form, but interestingly the quadrant is below the circle.

An important change occurred in Oliveros's work when she consciously used the mandala as the form of a composition. This happened in Meditation on the Points of the Compass (1970), commissioned by David Nott for the Illinois Wesleyan Choir. 22 Oliveros called her piece "an inter-religious, multi-lingual choral composition." She incorporated elements of meditation, theater, ritual, and ceremony. The compass is a mandala form symbolic of guiding and directing, and for Oliveros personally Meditation on the Points of the Compass literally turned her around and made her face new musical directions.

She used the compass as the seating arrangement for the performance space so that both audience and performers form a living mandala. A reduction of the score's title page diagrams this placement (see page 96).

In addition to the compass mandala, which is a visual meditation, several other meditations function within the piece: a beginning candle-lighting ceremony, a short meditation of three or four minutes in which everyone concentrates on breathing (the composer suggests the Yoga fourfold breathing technique23) and on the sounds of gongs, wind, buzzing, humming, and whistling, which are often associated with meditative practices. 24 The instrumentation comprises four Japanese bowl gongs, four Chinese gongs, and four temple blocks. There are twelve singer soloists (six male and six female divided into four solo groups, which Oliveros would like to represent a mixture of religious and racial backgrounds, such as Indian, Chicano, Asian or Hebrew, Catholic, Protestant, Agnostic, Atheist, etc.), and a large choir having small bells and finger cymbals. The audience is invited to participate and is shown the breathing meditation and how to perform its repertoire of wind sounds, humming or buzzing, whistling, and finally long tones of any pitch, the kind of meditative improvisation that Oliveros had been doing herself. The chorus also performs these sounds.

Gradually, by means of a simple cueing system, the

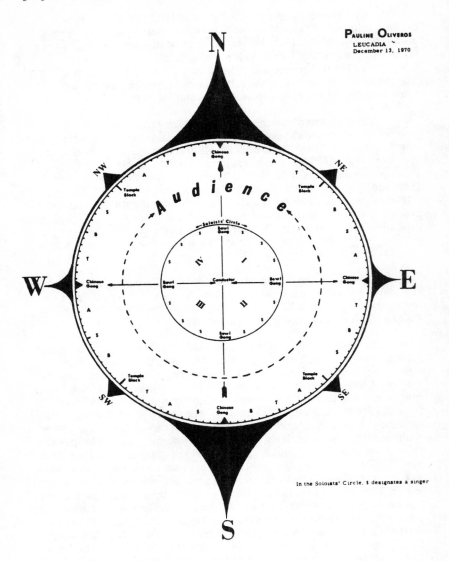

Mandala used in Meditation on the Points of the Compass.

entire compass becomes sonic, and once the texture of
gongs, audience, chorus, and temple blocks is established
the central mandala of soloists is heard. Each singer has
previously chosen a text portraying his or her religious belief and intones it according to specific directions. Rhythms
are derived from the text, and a Psalm tone is created
around the fundamental or partial of one of the bowl gongs.
The singers may depart from the fundamental and create
their own modes, but these must be one whole step above
or below the Psalm tone used. If performed correctly (and
this is not easy), each singer will be concentrating upon
preserving his or her Psalm tone. This kind of intensive
listening is a meditation in itself. The accuracy of the
performance depends upon how appropriate the text is to
each singer personally: the quality of the singer's choice
is heard in the quality of his or her sound.

One of the biggest changes that occurred with Meditation on the Points of the Compass is that the mood and
emotion of the piece stay constant. There is no drastic
split, as in Pieces of Eight, where the humorous Treasure
Island imagery is suddenly interrupted by the bust of Beethoven heading a collection ceremony, or where the strange
performance gestures in Aeolian Partitions are followed by
the telepathic meditation. There are few changes even in
sonic content, and events are leisurely paced to permit time
to listen, participate, and think.

Oliveros experimented even further with audience
participation in her next large meditative theatrical work,
Phantom Fathom (II) from the Theater of the Ancient Trumpeters: A Ceremonial Participation Evening (1972). It was
performed at the closing of her fellowship at the Center for
Music Experiment. The piece is a mix of many events: a
greeting meditation, dream ritual, snake dance, and silent
dinner. Oliveros made it clear to those attending what she
expected of them. On page 98 is a copy of the invitation
to participate; notice that the printing forms a mandala. The
reverse side offers explicit directions about the obligations
of being an audience member.

Phantom Fathom was not highly successful because
there were too many unrelated elements, too many phantoms
to comprehend. But the real phantom of the piece was Oliveros's attempt to communicate a particular sound and image
into the dream content of participating members. The instructions suggested that anyone who wanted to be part of the

You Are In vited To Participate

Phan in tom Fathom
_From the Theater of the Ancient
Trumpeters Sonic Med itation and
Ritual with the members of the
Meditation Project under the direction
of Pauline Oliveros and oc curring on Sat,
March 10 at 8:00 PM, 1973 in Room 408
Matthews Campus
Project for Music Experiment, UC San Diego
please see reverse side_

Invitation to attend <u>Phantom Fathom</u>.   Used by permission.

dream telepathy concentrate every night on the name Pauline
Oliveros or on a remembered image of her in an attempt to
make his or her dreams receptive to Oliveros's dream communication.   At the end of the performance it was revealed
that the image was a trumpeting elephant and the sound was
that of a conch shell, both of which appeared in some dream
imagery related during the dream ritual.

Both the elephant and the conch shell are significant
in Oliveros's later work.   The photograph on page 99, taken
by Becky Cohen, is by now a classic.   It shows Oliveros in
a meditative pose while seated atop an elephant, a mystic
symbol in Asian Indian culture.   Elephants are personally
symbolic to her; she says they appear in her dreams.   Oliveros also considers the crow to be her herald and totem
animal.   This is evident in her ceremonial opera <u>Crow
Two</u> (1975) and a later meditation, <u>Crow's Nest</u>, performed
at New York's Guggenheim Museum in 1979.

These symbols, experiences, and research studies
became sources of creative ideas as Oliveros began to realize that she was working with an interior tuning system, one

Photograph by Becky Cohen.   Used by permission.

in which performers are told how to listen and what should occupy their attention and awareness.   Oliveros was sensitive to external events and her own personal processing of sensations, thoughts, and emotions.   She began to explore these areas in her Sonic Meditations.   It took her several years to discover how to describe the interior actions that produced predictable outcomes.

Notes

1.   For more information about Ingber's work see Lester Ingber, Karate Kinematics and Dynamics (Hollywood, Calif.: Unique, 1981), and "Attention, Physics and Teaching," Journal for Social and Biological Studies, IV (1981), 225-235.

2.   For a survey of ritual and ceremony see Joseph Campbell, The Masks of God (New York: Viking Press, 1959, 4 vols.), The Hero with a Thousand Faces, 2nd ed. (Princeton, N.J.:   Princeton University Press, 1968), and Myths, Dreams and Religion (New York: Dutton, 1970).   Campbell is the editor of the latter book.

3.   Mircea Eliade, The Sacred and the Profane (New York: Harcourt, 1957); From Primitives to Zen (San Francisco: Harper and Row, 1977 paperback edition) is a compilation of some of his other works.

4.   Jerome Rothenberg, editor.   Technicians of the Sacred (New York: Doubleday, 1968).

5.   See Joseph Bogen's article "The Other Side of the Brain: An Appositional Mind" in Robert Ornstein, editor, The Nature of Human Consciousness (San Francisco: Freeman, 1973), pp. 101-125.

6.   For an example of Diana Deutsch's work see her abstract "Musical Illusions and Handedness," College Music Symposium, Spring 1980, p. 189.

7.   Roger Reynolds, Mind Models: New Forms of Musical Experience (New York: Praeger, 1975).

8.   Perspectives of New Music, XIX, 1 and 2, features "A San Diego-Centered Anthology," pp. 101-265, that describes the Center for Music Experiment.

9.   Ron Lane was supportive of the dream interpretation suggested by Calvin S. Hall, The Meaning of Dreams (New York: McGraw-Hill, 1966), and Robert Assagioli's creative use of imagery as described in The Act of Will (Baltimore: Penguin, 1973).

10.   Pauline Oliveros, in Numus West, April 1973, p. 36.

11.   Pauline Oliveros, "Three Themes, " Numus West, January 1972, pp. 8-11.

12.   Oliveros describes her karate lessons in "Many Strands, " Numus West, March 1975, pp. 6-12.

13.   Robert Ornstein, The Mind Field (New York: Simon and Schuster, 1976), p. 51.

14.   Ibid. , p. 35.

15.   Reprinted by permission.

16.   After the project Oliveros wrote "On Sonic Meditation," a report about her work.   A copy of this manuscript is available from the Center for Music Experiment, University of California at San Diego, La Jolla, CA 92093.   Her article in the Painted Bride Quarterly (see note 17) is a synopsis of this document.

17.   Pauline Oliveros, "On Sonic Meditation," The Painted Bride Quarterly, Winter 1976, pp. 54-69.   She also includes the scores to Meditations XII-XXV in this article.

18.   Oliveros, "On Sonic Meditation, " p. 54.

19.   This is from a copy of a grant proposal addressed to Dr. Paul Saltman, Vice Chancellor/Academic Affairs, dated February 12, 1975.   Used by permission.

20.   Carl Jung, Mandala Symbolism (Princeton, N.J.: Princeton University Press, 1972), p. v.

21.   This is one of Jung's last works.   See his Collected Works, vol. X, paragraph 803.

22.   Illinois Wesleyan has annually commissioned new choral works.

23.   See Richard Hittleman, Yoga (New York: Bantam, 1973), pp. 51-52.

24.   Oliveros intuitively chose to use these sounds without knowing that many of them are nadam, internally generated sounds used as meditation objects in the Yoga tradition. Claudio Naranjo discusses them in the book he co-authored with Robert Ornstein, On the Psychology of Meditation (New York: Viking, 1971), p. 153.

7: THE SONIC MEDITATIONS

Musicians are good candidates for meditation study because musical training is similar to that of meditation. John Cage, La Monte Young, Terry Riley, Stuart Dempster, and Anthony Newman have combined music and meditation in their work. The aftereffects of meditation are appealing. Psychologists and physiologists report that meditation can reduce heart rate, promote slower and deeper breathing, provide a healthy disruption of daily habitual patterns, and produce feelings of harmony and peace within oneself. These calming effects, especially the deep breathing, are immediately beneficial for the performer.

Also, as Ornstein and others have pointed out, artists often expose other consciousnesses, areas that can be reached through meditation. Carl Jung used the image of an artist as a prophet somehow aware of the future, and Ezra Pound said an artist possesses antennae that are sensitive to many phenomena. Composers can express aspects of contemporary culture through sound that would be very difficult to explain in ordinary language, and Claudio Naranjo, who has studied the spirit and techniques of meditation, writes, "My own experience of meditation shows me that the essence of meditation is also the essence of art...."[1]

Other composers in addition to Oliveros have written meditative pieces. Karlheinz Stockhausen's Mantra (1970), Hymnen (1969), Stimmung (1968), and especially Es und Aufwärts den Sieben Tagen (It and Upwards from the Seven Days) (1968) are in this genre. In Es und Aufwärts Stockhausen uses what he calls "intuitive playing";

[103]

the performer is to play only when not thinking or in a state
of nonthinking.   The directions are contradictory.   They
should be: "think about your playing. " It is curious that
the composer mentions on the record liner notes (Deutsche
Grammophon 2530 255) that the disc was made from the tape
of the first reading.   It is rather astonishing to hear a constant dense sonic texture, which should be interpreted as the
performers maintaining a state of nonthinking with very little practice, when just the opposite is expected.

Olivier Messiaen, the French composer, is greatly
misunderstood because listening to his work is actually a
meditation, and some audiences find repulsive the static and
what seem to be repetitive qualities of his music.   Frequently Messiaen includes inscriptions and subtitles to aid the listener in interpreting his compositions, often mentioning such
images as the Angel of the Apocalypse, the jewels of the
Heavenly City, or rainbows.   On several occasions I have
witnessed an entire audience becoming literally enraptured
by the sounds of his Quartet for the End of Time (1941).

John Cage, too, is often misunderstood.   Cage's
compositional use of chance, his philosophy that art and life
are the same, and particularly his famous piece of so-called
silence, 4'33" (1952), are strongly rooted in Zen tradition.
Having studied Zen with D. T. Suzuki, Cage demands that
performers have strict control over attention.   Many of his
pieces, such as Imaginary Landscape No. 4, for twelve
radios (1951), are meditations that measure the passing of
time.

Ben Johnston, known primarily for his microtonal
compositions, has also experimented with meditation.   In
Visions and Spells, a realization of Vigil (1976), he specifies a meditation period as a prerequisite for performance.

R. Murray Schafer, a Canadian, has explored intuitive music making.   His teaching techniques encourage students to develop clairaudience, what Schafer calls clean
hearing, which is somewhat akin to Oliveros's meditational
pieces.   Schafer's The Tuning of the World is a fascinating
study of environmental sound and cultural attitudes. 2

There are several reasons why Oliveros's Meditations
are unique.   Ever since Meditation on the Points of the Compass she has been investigating world religions and world music.   Music began to assume a political and social role in

her life. Music has power, but in the tradition of Western culture powerful people (such as members of the Church hierarchy, nobility, and patrons) controlled music. As a composer Oliveros wanted to provide an opportunity for everyone to make music.

Music has been a strong element in revolutionary and resistance movements, and for a short time Oliveros associated her Sonic Meditations with feminism. It is in the Source publication of the first twelve meditations that she publically stated that she was a lesbian, 3 but she soon abandoned the position of working solely with women and interpreted the term feminism in its broadest possible meaning, as demonstrated in her piece To Valerie Solanas and Marilyn Monroe in Recognition of Their Desperation----.

The Meditations are physically beneficial. Oliveros thought that her compositions could produce a calming effect and heightened states of awareness, a term she never really defined. 4

But the most important reason why the Meditations are so different is that Oliveros was evolving a new musical theory, as yet unnamed. I call it "sonic awareness." The term describes the ability consciously to focus attention upon environmental and musical sound. Sonic awareness is ideally characterized by a continual alertness to sound and an inclination to be always listening, much like John Berger's description of visual consciousness in his books About Looking and Ways of Seeing. 5

Oliveros has partially described her theory in the "Introductions" to her Sonic Meditations and in several published articles. Like all theories, sonic awareness can only be fully articulated after years of studying the medium (sound and time). As is often the case with creativity, it might appear synchronous with work done by others whose concerns are similar--for instance, Schafer and Stockhausen, whose meditative works have been mentioned earlier. Although Oliveros's theory is rooted in John Cage's investigations of change and indeterminacy, Cage's music and Oliveros's have little in common.

Sonic awareness is a perceptual theory about how we hear and make sounds. It is based upon two modes of human processing--focal attention and global attention. For Oliveros global attention is nonlinear and registers sensory,

imaged, and remembered information.   Focal attention is
occupied with single or sequential and linear material.   In
her recent lectures Oliveros has used the archetypal mandala symbolism of a circle with a centered dot as a model
of this relationship, with the circle representing global attention and the dot representing focal attention.   The symbol
is so important to her theory that it is often the structural

Archetypal mandala

and visual basis for many of her more recent pieces, such
as Rose Moon (1976) and El Relicario de los Animales (1979).

        Oliveros's sonic awareness is a synthesis of the psy-
chology of consciousness, the physiology of the martial arts,
and the sociology of the feminist movement.   The theory of
sonic awareness promotes sound that is easy to produce because it is often vocal; sound that is free from complicated
systems because the scores are in prose and the directions
can be easily memorized; and sound that is powerful in its
effects and in a compositional context where Western aesthetic principles of psychical distance and dichotomy between art
and nature are trespassed.   For Oliveros ritualism, cere-
monials, healing, and humanism become the goals of sonic
awareness and beauty the by-product.

        The theory generates complex sound masses possess-
ing a strong tonal center--these are normally conflicting
terms, but it is still an adequate description of the functions
of focal attention, which is tonal (single), and global attention, which registers surrounding material (the mass).   Timbre, attack, duration, intensity, and sometimes pitch are extremely flexible and often cover a wide gamut of possibilities.
Time and space, the freest of all dimensions, flaunt the musical tradition of formal body language (attitudes that Oliveros
opposed in her theater pieces) and acceptable concert schedul-
ing.   Long segments of time and environmental settings re-

place the Western concept of where and when music should
be performed.   This theory says that music should be for
everyone anywhere.

Sonic awareness can function as a complementary dimension of music theory.   Oliveros incorporated it into her
teaching of the undergraduate and graduate curriculum for
music students.   Disciplines other than music have already
considered new dimensions to their body of theoretical knowledge.   The physicist Niels Bohr introduced the principle of
complementarity to the scientific world when he discovered
that different modes of observation can produce differing and
not contradicting information about natural phenomena.   Bohr's
discovery that electrons behave as waves as well as the previously considered particles led to his formation of the principle of complementarity. 6

Discoveries in one area of thought are frequently reflected in other disciplines, a fact that Oliveros often pointed
out in her teaching.   It is curious that Arnold Schoenberg, a
contemporary of Bohr, was describing his intuitive struggle
to realize and articulate musically what he termed the "su-
preme law of comprehensibility." In the 1950s, when Bohr
and others were working with complementarity, Jung was
presenting the concept of synchronicity, which he described
as another way of knowing, and Cage was experimenting with
the theory of change and indeterminacy in music.   Actually,
Oliveros was working with synchronicity when she introduced
telepathic meditation in her Aeolian Partitions.

In the early 1970s Oliveros began to work seriously
in the area of sonic awareness.   The topic became a mandala of possibilities that she divided into a fourfold procedure
of hearing sound.   One could actively make sound, imagine
sound, listen to present sound, or remember past sound.
The relationship among these procedures forms a cross,
which when inserted in a circle produces Jung's viewfinder
archetype.   This model became the foundation for her Sonic
Meditations.   Each meditation uses either active or passive
listening and sound making and is so complex theoretically
that it requires a separate discussion and analysis.   Oliveros analyzed her first meditation, "Teach Yourself to Fly,"
in The Painted Bride Quarterly. 7 In order to show the scope
of the complete collection I have made an index describing
each Meditation's sonic procedure, the tuning involved, and
an evaluation of how difficult the meditation would be for a
beginning group. 8

actively make sound

listen to present
sound ——————————————————————— remember past
sound

actually imagine sound

Fourfold procedure of hearing sound

     I.   "Teach Yourself to Fly"--focal and global atten-
tion tuned to breathing resulting in involuntary sounds; actually making sound; good for beginners.

     II.   Untitled--same tunings and procedure as above
but added awareness of ambiance and environment since performers are directed to search for particular kinds of space;
good for beginners.

     III.   "Pacific Tell"--focal attention tuned to mental
sound image while global attention switches from the active
to passive modes; actively imagining and actually making
sounds; difficult due to telepathy.

     IV.   Untitled--"Pacific Tell" performed with tape
recorders.   Same as above.

     V.   "Native"--solo meditation involving focal and
global attention to silent walking; listening to present sound;
excellent for everyone.

     VI.   "Sonic-Rorschach"--focal attention to technology
and global attention to own brain technology; listening to
present sound; concentration difficult for beginners.

     VII.   "Removing the Demon or Getting Your Rocks
Off"--focal attention to premeditated word and global attention to slow tempo; actually making sound; medium difficulty.

     VIII.   "Environmental Dialogue"--global attention to
environmental sounds and focal attention to reinforcing parts

of the sounds; listening to present sounds and actually making sounds; good for beginners; variations available for more advanced meditators.

IX. "The Greeting"--focal attention to constant tone and global attention to audience entrances; listening to present sound, actually making sounds, and actively imagining sounds; medium difficulty.

X. Untitled--focal attention to mental image of each performer and global attention to singing a tone to that person; actually making sounds; medium difficulty.

XI. "Bowl Gong"--focal attention to pitch of bowl gong and global attention to length of tonal memory; listening to present sounds and remembering sounds; difficult.

XII. "One Word"--focal attention to a word and global attention to its sound and speed; actually making sounds; difficult.

XIII. "Energy Changes"--focal attention to the environment and global attention to trigger and breath of resulting sound; listening to present sounds and actually making sounds; medium difficulty.

XIV. "Tumbling Song"--focal attention to vocal sound and global attention to descending gestures; actually making sounds; excellent for beginners.

XV. "Zina's Circle"--focal attention to breathing and global attention to trigger; actually making sounds; excellent for beginners.

XVI. Untitled--focal attention to tuning and global attention to time; actually making sounds; good for beginners.

XVII. "Ear Ly"--focal attention to tuning and global attention to trigger; listening to present sounds and actually making sounds; extremely difficult.

XVIII. "Re Cognition"--focal attention to listening and global attention to source; listening to present sound; medium difficulty.

XIX. Untitled--focal attention to internal sound and global attention to sight and sound; listening to present sound; good for beginners.

XX.   "Your Voice"--focal attention to your voice and global attention to its qualities; actively imagining sounds and remembering sounds; good for beginners.

XXI.   Untitled--focal attention to and global attention to the musical universe; remembering sounds; good for beginners.

XXII.   Untitled--focal attention to familiar sound and global attention to multiplicity of sound and its effect; actively imagining sound and remembering sound; excellent for beginners.

XXIII.   "Pure Noise"--focal attention to vocal tone and global attention to timbre; actually making sound and listening to present sound; medium difficulty.

XXIV.   Untitled--focal awareness of constant sound and global attention to imagined alternate sounds; listening to present sound and actively imagining sounds; medium difficulty.

XXV.   "Your Name--The Signature Meditation"-- focal attention to your name and global attention to its visual qualities; no sound is involved; medium difficulty.

Most of the Meditations are for voice, although several can be translated into instrumental sound.   Oliveros suggests the use of a tape recorder for some of her Meditations, and in these cases she treats the tape recorder as if it were an extension of the ear, a technique she had discovered during her early years in San Francisco.

Like all of her scores since 1961, the Sonic Meditations are in prose form and are explained in short, clear statements.   Each score must be carefully studied and constantly checked to ensure that the correct interpretation is being followed, because performers often try to substitute something different, an idea of their own that the Meditations might have suggested to them. [9]   This upsets the structure, since each Meditation has its own specific tunings that yield controlled and predictable musical results.

For this reason the Meditations are not improvisations that allow performers freedom to play with the dynamic elements.   There are no lines of communication established among members of a group to signal a chain of cause

and effect, such as a player imitating and expanding
upon a previous gesture. In fact the performers must
discard all thoughts except the directions of the Meditation.
Any distractions, such as a cueing system, hinder the process.

The Meditations have several compositional traits in
common. Oliveros uses three basic forms: variations,
open form (no specified ending), and closed form (a composed cadence). Nine of the twenty-five Meditations are
variations, a technique used in her earlier music. Oliveros
suggests alternative procedures that do not affect the basic
structure but often introduce an added complexity, such as
squeezing the hand-impulse in "Zina's Circle" to the left
rather than to the right.

In most of the Meditations the duration of the breath
determines the length of the gestures, so phrases tend to
become longer as the Meditation progresses. This is particularly noticeable in Meditations I, II, and XVI. After
some time has elapsed the phrases often become drones.

Several Meditations specify a tempo or time element.
"Removing the Demon or Getting Your Rocks Off" requires
that each person begin the meditation by mentally establishing a tempo as slow as possible and then sounding that tempo with a pair of resonant rocks.

This kind of mentally imagined organic tempo is
characteristic of Oliveros's percussion parts. She had to
experiment with the instructions in order to obtain the sound
she wanted. She discusses this dilemma in her article
"Single Stroke Roll Meditation (1973)."[10] Oliveros wanted
the percussion players to perform a clean and continuing
roll where different partials would gradually be heard and
the slow changes within all the sonic parameters would produce "an overall subtly shifting sound, hypnotic in its effect."[11] Her original instructions were: "choose one instrument which you like. Perform a single stroke roll until 'it
rolls.'"[12] She discovered, however, that this notation permitted all kinds of improvisatory situations. What she really needed to do was to give instructions that would bring
about an altered mode of consciousness. She stated:

> I needed a set of instructions which would prevent
> the player from the distraction or temptation of
> conscious changes in dynamics, rate and quality.

After many different attempts the instructions have evolved to the following: Each percussionist chooses a single instrument to be played with hands or mallets.   Each percussionist must first imagine the sound of his or her instrument: the rate, intensity and quality of the single stroke roll.   The actual roll must begin involuntarily as a result of imagining it.   Then, the task of meditation is to keep the actual roll matching the original imaginary roll for the duration of the performance. 13

Another interesting time study is "Bowl Gong," in which meditators strike a Japanese bowl gong and concentrate on mentally maintaining the pitch of the gong.   When someone loses this pitch then the person restrikes the gong. This is just the opposite situation to Stockhausen's Es und Aufwärts, in which the composer wants musicians to sound their state of nonthinking.

As in her participation instructions for the meditation research project, Oliveros explains in the "Introduction" to the Sonic Meditations that performers must be willing to commit themselves to certain conditions, such as regular meetings.   Implicit in these meetings is the need for a leader to ensure that the directions are being followed.   The leader needs to be someone with meditative experience.   In terms of mandala theory the leader provides the center. This presence of a leader is so important that frequently Oliveros travels to do workshops about her Sonic Meditations.   Sometimes she forms a core group that meets two or three days before a performance, and at other times she immediately involves the audience in performing several meditations.

Often Oliveros uses "Teach Yourself to Fly" as a starter meditation, and I find that it is an excellent example of how the Sonic Meditations are music.   The "score" reads:

Any number of persons sit in a circle facing the center.   Illuminate the space with dim blue light. Begin by simply observing your own breathing. Always be an observer.   Gradually allow your breathing to become audible.   Then gradually introduce your voice.   Allow your vocal cords to vibrate in any mode which occurs naturally.   Al-

low the intensity to increase very slowly. Continue
as long as possible naturally, and until all others
are quiet, always observing your own breath cycle.[14]

"Teach Yourself to Fly" is musically satisfying because the tuning for focal attention and global attention is
obvious and simple and the sonic procedure of making sounds
produces complex results. If both focal and global attention
are centered upon only observing the breath, then it is easy
just to allow the vocal cords to vibrate. The performer is
relaxed and without such thoughts as "I wonder if I can do
this?" "I can't sing." "What will I sound like?" "Who is
going to make the first sound?" Breathing will have slowed
down and become deeper, the vocal cords will involuntarily
begin to vibrate. The kinds of sounds that naturally emerge
are long drones that come and go like waves. These are
the only sounds that can occur if the directions are followed.
As soon as the involuntary aspect of just allowing and observing the vocal cords vibrating is abandoned, then the
sounds will abruptly change. If one person consciously begins to manipulate the sound, such as imitating the sounds
that someone else is making, then the Meditation is destroyed and becomes improvisation.

These compositions are easily sabotaged. I have
noticed that inexperienced musicians and nonmusicians perform the Meditation beautifully. They follow directions.
The more sophisticated musicians find this difficult and frequently begin to manipulate. This is because musicians are
taught to control sound, a tendency that is especially noticeable when trained singers are part of the group. Their
manicured sounds are inappropriate and appear dissonant in
this context. The difficulty lies in asking musicians to de-
tach themselves from their training so that they can accept
certain freedoms: no parts to read, so that musical notation is not a concern; generally no visual triggers for sound,
so that there is no need to follow a conductor; no audience
to delight, so that there is no opportunity to experience the
nervousness or thrill of performing; no specific musical system, so that there is no prescribed time and pitch manipula-
tions and no familiar and comfortable patterns; and no anxiety
over anticipating what should happen next, so who can fail?

The aftereffects of "Teach Yourself to Fly" are interesting to observe. Oliveros claims that the Meditations can
heighten global attention and extend consciousness. If, as
she believes, global attention is the property of the sensory

modes, then these are some ways that global attention is heightened: discovering that one can sing and produce long steady tones; learning to expand the breathing cycle;[15] hearing and making subtle increments in an intensity scale (the piece begins almost at the threshold of audibility and can peak at a very intense loudness level); and realizing that sounds seem to blend together naturally and form a complex whole.   These discoveries can be endless, depending upon the experience of the individual, and happen as a by-product of performing "Teach Yourself to Fly."

The concept of "expanded consciousness" is more difficult to analyze.   If one considers consciousness to be selective, then an expanded consciousness is one that can take in more selection.   Being in and prolonging the state of observing one's own involuntary action is often an unfamiliar mode, but I think a crucial extension of consciousness is realizing that making beautiful music is not the sole property of musicians.   For those who are classically trained (the person who has studied piano for twelve years, and so on) this is a consciousness-raising experience.   The symbolism in the title "Teach Yourself to Fly" is most appropriate.

Other Meditations are more difficult.   In "Pacific Tell" sounds are actively imagined and mentally maintained without sonic feedback.   Oliveros frequently uses an exercise to demonstrate how hard it is to keep focal and global attention tuned to an imagined sound.   She sets a kitchen timer for a relatively short interval, say, less than three minutes.   The timer needs a bell mechanism, like the Lux Minutes Minder, rather than a buzz alarm.   Once the timer is set, the instructions are:

> Listen to everything you can possibly hear both externally from the environment and internally from the memory, imagination, or internal environment (i.e. body sounds).   Allow your attention to expand to include the most distant and faintest sounds without premeditating a pitch.   When the cue comes respond as instantly as possible with a pitch that matches one sounding externally or internally at the moment.

The promptitude of the sung response mirrors the quality of attention.   Most people's experience is that attention wanders from the tone and all kinds of vagrant thoughts appear, a condition that Zen teaching calls "the monkey mind." The sounding of the bell is the sensory input for awareness (ideally attention is globally accepting sensory input while waiting for the one event, the bell, that will cue the vocal cords to sound the content of attention).

"Pacific Tell" uses a form of telepathy in which information is sent and received without the customary sensory channels. The score reads:

> Find your place in a darkened space or a deserted out-of-doors area. Mentally form a sound image. Assume that the magnitude of your concentration on, or the vividness of this sound image will cause one or more of the group to receive this sound image by telepathic transmission. Visualize the person to whom you are sending. Rest after your attempted telepathic transmission by becoming mentally blank. When or if a sound image different from your own forms in your mind, assume that you are receiving from someone else, then make that sound image audible. Rest again by becoming mentally blank or return to your own mental sound image. Continue as long as possible or until all others are quiet. 16

Besides trying to imagine sound actively, there is the problem of becoming mentally blank. An added difficulty in "Pacific Tell" is switching from sending a sound image via one's own concentration to becoming receptive to receiving someone else's sound image. This involves a form of telepathy, certainly an undeveloped skill for most people. Actually, telepathy is a process of self-observation, a test of trust in one's intuitive mode, and should be included in the theory of sonic awareness as a complementary mode of hearing.

"Pacific Tell" requires that focal attention be extremely active while global attention is hardly functioning. It is even possible that one might not hear other members sound the received sounds, so in that case there is no feedback process at all.

Another equally difficult meditation is "The Greeting," which features a complex relationship between focal and global attention. Sounds are both made and imagined. The score reads:

> Informed persons should begin the greeting at least
> half-an-hour or more before a scheduled meeting
> or program.   After you are seated and comfortable,
> allow a tone to come into mind.   Keep returning
> your attention to this same tone.   Everytime a
> person or persons enter this space, greet them by
> singing the tone, as you were greeted when you
> entered this space.   Continue this meditation until
> all are present. 17

The stark simplicity of "The Greeting" is hard to
maintain because its sonic realization demands the utmost
precision.   The pitch content must always be the same (even
though duration may change) and the ensemble coordination of
attack and cutoff must be exact.   The success or failure of
these conditions is dependent upon the meditator's consciousness of his or her own natural voice.   In her article "On
Sonic Meditation" Oliveros observed that trained singers apply a filter to their voices; they are taught to produce certain kinds of sounds and to eliminate qualities that are
thought to be undesirable.   On the other hand, musicians
who are not singers are hardly aware of their voices and
often find singing embarrassing.   This lack of attention to
the natural voice is a pity, and it is lucky when a musician
discovers his or her own voice by accident.   When Oliveros
wrote "The Greeting," she was beginning to realize the musical consequences of finding one's voice.   The following
words of Inayat Khan, a Sufi musician whose book Music
Oliveros owns, may have been the inspiration for this
Meditation:

> Every person, whether he knows it or not, has a
> predilection for a certain sound.   Although most
> people do not study this subject and therefore man
> usually remains ignorant of this idea, yet every
> person has his note.   The fact is that each per-
> son has his sound, a sound which is akin to his
> particular evolution.   Besides all the divisions that
> have been made such as tenor, bass or baritone,
> each person has his particular pitch and each per-
> son has his special note on which he speaks, and
> the particular note is expressive of his life's evo-
> lution, expressive of his soul, of the condition of
> his feelings and of his thoughts. 18

If the Sonic Meditation Group has been meeting regu-
larly, members will certainly have made some discoveries

about their own voice and might very well have located their "certain sound." The more natural the tone is that is allowed to come to mind for "The Greeting," the more exact will be each repetition.

Breath control is another difficulty, since the duration of the sound is determined by when and how people enter. The score is ambiguous about when the sound is to stop. I interpret the cutoff to be when an entering person is settled in the space. Again, the ensemble precision is proportioned to the balance between focal and global attention. It is possible that toward the end of the meditation (which is specified as beginning about half an hour previous to another scheduled event) there will be so many entrances that "The Greeting" will be sounding continuously for several minutes. If the score has been properly followed, the meditators' breathing rate and depth should support the prolonged tones.

Ensemble balance might also be another problem where one or two members' tones would be louder than the others. This is an unlikely situation, however, because the degree of awareness demanded precludes any person or persons from dominating; one would immediately sense the lack of balance and make adjustments, and as a result an exquisite mix occurs that would be the envy of a woodwind or brass section.

Even if the meditators have not realized their own natural sound, and the performance is not perfect, "The Greeting" is beautiful, especially when listeners realize that their entrance triggers sound.

"The Environmental Dialogue" is a much simpler meditation because global attention is stabilized while focal attention is free to scan the contents of auditory input. Listening is accompanied by sonic or mental reinforcement. The two procedures are listening to present sounds and making sound. The score reads:

> Each person finds a place to be, either near or distant from the others either indoors or out-of-doors. Begin the meditation by observing your own breathing. As you become aware of sounds from the environment, gradually begin to reinforce the pitch of the sound source. Reinforce either vocally, mentally or with an instrument. If you

lose touch with the source, wait quietly for another. Reinforce means to strengthen or sustain.
If the pitch of the sound source is out of your
range, then reinforce it mentally.[19]

Conscientious performers can intuitively discover information about the nature of sound. Attention requires that
the person imitate the frequency, amplitude, attack, timbre,
and duration (when appropriate) of the sounds perceived.
Often performers find that they can extend the high and low
ends of their vocal ranges in order to reinforce the sounds
they are hearing. In addition a person soon realizes that
sounds are complex and it is quite possible to reinforce
only a partial of a very rich environmental sound.

"The Environmental Dialogue" is an excellent study
in envelope shapes and phrasing. No matter how static the
sound, one can hear subtle internal changes, and the overlapping of one sound upon another produces a variety of
sonic mixes. Compositionally, what-happens-when is fascinating. There are no boring moments when listening to
these environmental sounds in a musical context. This supports Naranjo's observation that meditation is not something
separate or even different from other things. "The Environmental Dialogue" is musical meditation and meditational music.

Although the Sonic Meditations were a dramatic change
for Oliveros, they inherited some evolutionary aspects from
her previous work. For instance, almost all of the Meditations assume a theatrical appearance. Many use a circular
formation, and her future meditations become visual mandalas as well. Several of the Meditations require specific
kinds of places, such as "a natural or artificial canyon,
forest or deserted municipal quad" (Meditation II), "the separation of a distance that might be great, i.e., thousands of
miles or light years" (Meditation IV), Lake Winnepausaukee
for "Environmental Dialogue for the New Hampshire Festival
Orchestra" (a variation of Meditation VIII), and many require
a setting in which one can hear environmental sounds--an
invitation to perform in the sonically rich out-of-doors.

Most of the Meditations specify some kind of lighting,
usually low illumination, dim blue light, or eyes closed.
Photo lamps or strobe lights are sometimes used as a time
signal.

Some of Oliveros's more recent compositions, such as Crow Two and Rose Moon, combine various meditations into more specific theater settings. These pieces require an intensely trained ensemble and are staged as a performance with an audience. They are discussed in the following chapter.

Notes

1.   Claudio Naranjo and Robert Ornstein, On the Psychology of Meditation (New York: Viking, 1971), p. 27.   For more information about meditation and music see Tom Johnson, "Meditate on Sound," Village Voice, May 24, 1976.

2.   R. Murray Schafer, The Tuning of the World (New York: Knopf, 1977).

3.   Pauline Oliveros, "Sonic Meditations," Source, V, 2 (1971), 103-107.

4.   Pauline Oliveros, "Introduction I," Sonic Meditations, published by Smith Publications, 1974.

5.   John Berger, About Looking (New York: Pantheon, 1980) and Ways of Seeing (New York: Penguin, 1977).

6.   For a simplified explanation of Bohr's principle of complementarity see Thomas R. Blackburn, "Sensuous-Intellectual Complementarity in Science," Robert Ornstein, editor, The Nature of Human Consciousness (San Francisco: Freeman, 1973), pp. 27-40.   Fritjof Capra also discusses Bohr's work in The Tao of Physics (New York: Bantam, 1977).

7.   Pauline Oliveros, "On Sonic Meditation," The Painted Bride Quarterly, Winter 1976, p. 54.

8.   The Sonic Meditations are ordered according to date of composition.   I am making the judgment about difficulty based upon six years of using some of the Meditations in a classroom and two years of working with a sonic-meditation group that met weekly for two or more hours.

9.   Peter Hamel succumbs to this temptation in his book Through Music to the Self (Boulder, Colo.:   Shambhala,

1979), p. 202, when he transforms Zina's Circle into an exercise of his own. Hamel, however, does acknowledge Oliveros's work.

10. Pauline Oliveros, "Single Stroke Roll Meditation (1973)," Percussionist, XII (Spring 1975), 109-110. Reprinted by permission of the publisher.

11. Ibid., p. 109.

12. Ibid.

13. Ibid.

14. Oliveros, Sonic Meditations, meditation I. Reprinted by permission of the publisher.

15. See Aldous Huxley, Heaven and Hell (New York: Harper, 1954), pp. 144-145, for his explanation of how breath control functions in extended states of consciousness.

16. Sonic Meditations, meditation III. Reprinted by permission of the publisher.

17. Ibid., meditation IX. Reprinted by permission of the publisher.

18. Sufi Knayat Khan, Music (New Delhi: Sufi Publishing, 1962), p. 74.

19. Sonic Meditations, meditation VIII. Reprinted by permission of the publisher.

After completing <u>Sonic Meditations</u>, Oliveros received several boosts in her career. First, she was awarded a fellowship from the John Simon Guggenheim Foundation to study ritualism in American Indian music.   This coincided with a commission from the State University of New York at Buffalo.   Next she was awarded tenure as associate professor at the University of California at San Diego.   A short time later she was asked to be a member of the composer/librettist panel for the National Endowment for the Arts. These honors added weight to her reputation as a radical artist.   In addition her experience with reviewing grant applications for the National Endowment for the Arts gave her wide exposure to what composers were writing and convinced Oliveros to continue in the direction of meditation, an area in which she felt her music was both interesting and humanistic.

The Guggenheim fellowship gave her time to study myth and ritual.   The scholarship of Jung, Campbell, and Eliade, as well as Rothenberg's anthologies of primitive poetry, affected her work.   Oliveros began to make distinctions. She carefully avoided calling her compositions rituals because "ritual" connotes a belief system that maintains established myths.   She preferred the term "ceremony," something that is less structured, although acts are prescribed.   For Oliveros's purposes ceremonies provided a context in which she could write theater pieces using her personal visual and sonic imagery and oral tradition.   Also, use of the term "ceremony" encouraged audience participation and that of amateurs and nonmusicians, a direction that appealed to her.

[121]

Her ceremonies needed structure, however, and Oliveros realized that since mandalas promoted visual awareness they could easily be incorporated in her theory of sonic awareness. Because mandalas were psychograms, messages from the psyche, they were related to her use of primary process imagery. Her imagined improvisation, Beethoven symbolism, compasses, elephants, and crows were psychograms, and the circular mandala has become the primary psychogram and logo of her later works.

The meaning of psychogram can be enlarged to include a coined word, "psychosonics"--literally, sounds of the psyche or mental life of the individual. Some of the Sonic Meditations, the sound of the conch shell, sounds received during dreams, and imagined sounds are psychosonic. Oliveros has always been attracted to the sacred power of sound in shamanism, Tibetan Buddhism, and Sufism, all examples of psychosonics.

Many contemporary painters, weavers, and photographers feature mandala images in their art. José and Miriam Argüelles have written a book about such work.[1] Carl Sagan's popular Cosmos reproduces mandala forms that scientists have discovered, although Sagan never uses the term "mandala."[2]

The Argüelleses have discussed the modular aspects of mandala forms and describe them as "exhibiting principles of ... resonance and synchronicity,"[3] musical characteristics that Oliveros employed in her Sonic Meditations. In her larger works meditations are overlaid--for example, percussionists perform "The Single Stroke Roll" while someone else is concentrating on "Energy Changes"--and there are elaborate designs for staging, costuming, and lighting. Yet all elements are resonant with the mandala's psychogram.

Mandala time is based upon the principle of synchronicity: events do not develop in the Western sense of linear cause and effect. Mandala ceremonies take generous amounts of time, often a difficult listening situation because the Western culture is relatively inexperienced in perceiving psychosonics.

Mandalas also provided Oliveros with opportunities for collaboration with others, an aspect of her work that she has cultivated through the years. She controls the idea of the composition but delegates to her friends the responsibility for designing costumes, lighting, staging, movement, and props.

Crow Two (1975) is an example of this kind of col-laboration. It was an important piece for her, commis-sioned by the State University of New York at Buffalo with funds provided by the National Endowment for the Arts. Oliveros composed the piece during a leave of absence that was supported by her Guggenheim fellowship. During this time Oliveros studied bird symbolism in Indian rituals and ceremonies and noticed that a group of crows frequented her Leucadia property. In the spirit of her research she adopted the crow as her herald and totem, making it the psychogram for her mandala.

Many people were involved in Crow Two's premiere, which celebrated the opening of the Mandeville Center at the University of California, San Diego. (An earlier version, called Crow, was performed at Buffalo.) As in many of her pieces, Oliveros had personal reasons, in addition to the fellowship and commission, for composing Crow Two. She wanted to commemorate her grandmother's recent death and to feature Al Huang, Julius Eastman, a young singer, and Margaret Porter, a poet friend. Oliveros felt strong loyalty toward her grandmother, Pauline Gribbin, which she needed to express. She included four women as a silent module in the inner circle of her mandala for Crow Two. The women each represented a mother figure, a tribal idea in harmony with the piece's Indian spirit.

The mandala form of the composition, which Oliveros calls a ceremonial opera, is another compass. The circle is outlined by seated meditators, named crow friends (re-placing the operatic chorus). The cardinal points are marked by the four women designated as crow mother west, crow stepmother east, crow grandmother south, and crow god-mother north. In the center is crow poet, who leisurely smokes a cigarette. In the Mandeville performance John Forkner, a visual artist, produced a luminic meditation of changing patterns of circles, crosses, and triangles.

Among the other personnel are a crow family, did-jeridu players, two mirror meditators, an energy changer, seven percussionists, two luminic meditators, and three crow heyokas (sacred clownlike figures from Sioux Indian rituals). Huang, Eastman, and Philip Larsen, a fellow at the Center for New Music, were the heyokas for the Mande-ville performance.

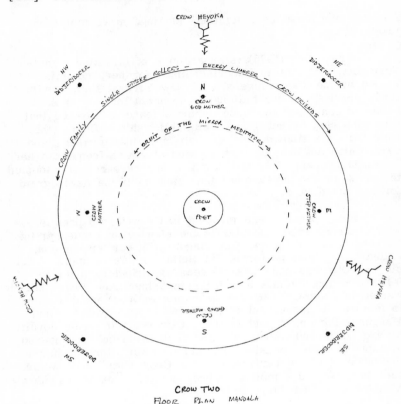

CROW TWO
FLOOR   PLAN   MANDALA

Mandala for Crow Two.   Forthcoming from Smith Publications.   Used by permission.

Oliveros includes Margaret Porter's poem "Crowlogue" in the program notes so that the audience can think about the universal symbolism of a crow before the performance starts.

> A crow is not a crow is a crow.   A crow,
> Bright-black, flashes through a sun-crazed field
>   of Van Gogh
> Or, raven, intones "Nevermore" in the chamber of
>   Poe
> From the bust of Pallas, as Athena's sacred bird,
> For whom, when needed, she would utter an ominous word.

Messenger, bird of beginnings, it was Crow who
    emerged
First of all from the Ark, Three-legged, Crow sits
    before
The sun-disk--Yang emblem of the Chinese Emperor.
Crow is chess-piece, the Rook; also, is seen to soar
In the constellation Corvus of the skies down-under.
To the Absaroke, "Bird-People," the bird of Thunder,
In sundry ages and places, a bird of wonder,
Crow is symbol of earth, of spirit, of maternal might.
Her caw makes part of the divination rite.
"As the crow flies" you go for the most direct flight.
What she steals she hoards and hides, and you never
    know
What havoc this omnivorous creature, as a pet, will
    sow.
Yet only a human being can be said to "eat crow."[4]

    Crow Two begins quietly while a circle of silent med-
itators, percussionists, didjeridu players, and telepathic flute
improvisors start their individual meditations. The mirror
meditators move slowly and orbit around the crow poet while
occasionally the energy changer injects percussive sounds.
After this static texture is firmly established, the heyokas
enter and try to disturb the meditators by performing dis-
tracting and exaggerated actions and sounds. Al Huang was
an especially dramatic heyoka. He wore a large black cape,
swirled a stick in the air, and shouted, but he was never
successful in interfering with the meditations. At last a
crow totem, a kitelike object made of mylar, lures him and
the other heyokas away. Crows are supposed to be attracted
to bright and shiny objects, and as old crows themselves the
heyokas finally leave the meditators alone.

    The audience hears a continuous drone of drumming
and didjeridu sounds, what the Indians call a "sound ground,"
that generates a serious mood that listeners find difficult to
tolerate unless they actually participate in the meditative
spirit. The heyokas are entertaining, but they perform only
for a short time. The essence of Crow Two is a meditative
ceremony that exposes members of an audience to a noncriti-
cal and nondevelopmental mode of listening. If they are receptive to the sounds and begin to hear all of the changes
among the partials and overtones of the various drones, then
Crow Two becomes relaxing and can change how a person
feels. If anyone cannot or will not listen in this manner,
then the composer prefers that he or she leave the performance,[5] which many people did. This does not bother Oliveros:

"Music should tune the soul, not merely entertain.   And I might add that in the tuning process it might fail as an object of admiration which is a risk I'm willing to take."[6]

In 1977 Oliveros received two commissions, one from Wesleyan University in Middletown, Connecticut, for a choral piece and the other from the Experimental Intermedia Foundation in New York City.   For the Wesleyan commission she composed another ceremony, Rose Moon (1977), which was performed by the Wesleyan singers as part of their 1978 tour.

The mandala for Rose Moon, even more elaborate than Crow Two's, is the performance setup, structure, and symbolism of the piece.   The mandala is at least twenty-five feet in diameter.   Previous to the performance the shape is marked out with tape (whitewash if the space is outdoors).   Linda Montano designed the costumes.   A large, circular, half-black and half-white tent is placed in the center of the circle.   The circle is divided into a compass and inside quadrants.   The lunatics (shown outside of the circle) are similar to the heyokas in Crow Two.

The performance of Rose Moon lasts for about two hours.   Its most compelling feature is the physical stamina and beauty of two runners who alternate for half-hour periods running counterclockwise around the circumference of the mandala, each runner maintaining the steady tempo that was established at the beginning of the piece.   The runners wear sounding belts made of bells, which amplify the sound of their running tempo.

The musicians are asked to perform simple but demanding tasks of concentration.   Eight performers, called cuers, sit in half-lotus position on pillows marking the circle's compass.   Never moving from this position, they sound their chosen percussion instrument each time they feel the runner pass their spine.   The runner's path is directly behind the cuers; so, providing that there are no lapses in attention or pace, the cuers and runner create an ostinato tempo that should remain constant for the entire duration of Rose Moon.

Inside the circle of cuers is a slowly moving clockwise procession of seven people led by the sound of the moon rattle, a spherical object made of papier-mâché and dried beans that is half-black and half-white.   The leader shakes

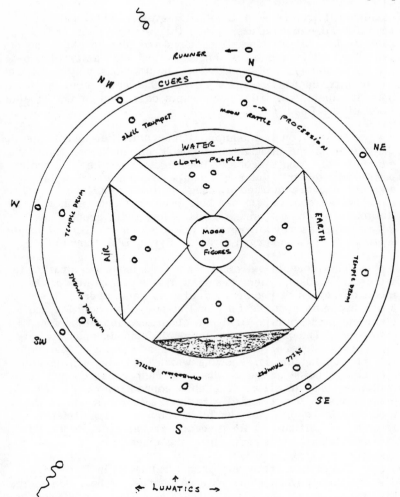

Mandala for Ro se Moon. Copyright 1977 by Smith Publications. Used by permission.

the rattle in tempo with the runner, and different cycles of
the procession are marked by giving the moon rattle to another performer, the rattle's sound and tempo never being
interrupted. The members of the procession carry exotic
instruments, such as two Japanese temple drums, two

conch-shell trumpets, a Cambodian rattle, and a pair of
wrathful Tibetan cymbals, which they sound at the end of
each cycle.   At all times the cuers are free to chant the
word "moon" in numerous languages and the names of people they want remembered.   The simultaneous playing of the
exotic instruments produces a sound that resembles the thigh-
bone trumpets, cymbals, and drums described in the Tibetan
Book of the Dead. 7

   Rose Moon is modular.   Other activities take place in
the center of the mandala.   A couple called "moon figures"
enter the tent and disrobe.   Twelve cloth people take their
position in the triangular quadrants called water, earth, air,
and fire and are marked by large colored cloth sheets.   The
cloth people concentrate on their breathing and begin a meditation in which they sing chords within their group.   At
specified times certain actions are performed with the large
cloths.   The choreography was by Sylvia D'Arcangelo.

   The piece is extremely slow and the concentration is
intense.   Audience members may also chant names of the
moon or names of people they wish to remember.   Rose
Moon becomes hypnotic for the listener who stays for the
complete performance, truly an endurance marathon for
everyone.   The physical and musical demands upon the cuers, processioners, and runners are staggering.   Maintaining the running tempo, knowing which cycle is in progress,
and always being aware of when the runner passes can be
prolonged only in states of intense concentration.   Little im-
perfections in tempo and discrepancies in the sound of the
moon rattle become obvious to the concentrating listener.
It would be difficult to imagine any choral group other than
the Wesleyan Singers performing the piece.

   There are, however, structural flaws in Rose Moon.
The mandala psychogram lacks resonance.   The moon waxes
and wanes, but most of the activities in Rose Moon are constant and the moon symbolism seems to have nothing to do
with the marathon concentration.   Normally the moon is considered a feminine symbol, but the man and woman in the
tent (Neeley Bruce and his wife) suggest a homogeneous sexual symbol, not the homosexual overtones that militant feminism often associates with moon symbolism.   Even the runners were female and male.

   Oliveros has personal reasons for using the title
Rose Moon.   Part of the symbolism is a reference to Linda

Montano, Oliveros's partner. At one time Montano went by
the name of Rose Mountain, a title Oliveros used for another
of her compositions. Also, the sounds and concentration of
the piece are very Tibetan. Oliveros even suggests that a
Lama or other spiritual protector participate in the procession, although she usually leads the performance herself. It
was at this time that she became interested in Tibetan Buddhist ritual and met the XVIth Gyalwa Karmapa, head of the
Kagyüpa lineage of Tibetan Buddhist teachers. He performed
the Black Crown Ceremony under the auspices of the Music
Department at the University of California, San Diego. Oliveros accepted the blessing for the department.

In Crow Two and Rose Moon Oliveros designed her
own mandala using symbols and imagery that were personally relevant to her. In the Yellow River Map (1977), commissioned by the Intermedia Foundation and composed and
premiered before Rose Moon, Oliveros used the ancient "Yellow River Map," said to have been the origins of the principles of the I Ching. 8 In collaboration with Al Huang she designed a piece that consisted of twelve activities called ritual
sequences. Oliveros abandoned her usual detailed and pre-
cise prose directions and instead prescribed a series of activities that would be difficult to recreate from the sparse
directions that are given in the published score. 9 Since The
Yellow River Map is a translation of the mandala into sound
and movement, rather than an imagined and composed performance, Oliveros could call her work a ritual and overtly
use the philosophical system of the I Ching.

Another commission in 1978, this time from the Independent Composers Association in Los Angeles, prompted
her to create a mandala piece whose very title is the mandala. The figure is a three-tiered spiral and eight spokes
marked out with masking tape, black cushions, and votive
candles. Four B♭ clarinets are positioned at the cardinal
points around the spiral; eight crystal glasses form the
spokes that emanate from the center, where a large bass
drum is played by four percussionists. A solo chanter,
having a pair of Tibetan finger cymbals and wearing two
cyalume chemical lights around her wrists, chants a text
in her native language (preferably foreign). She slowly
makes three transits in a spiral path around the drum
while the drummers independently perform "The Single
Stroke Roll."

The glasses are tuned to the first twelve overtones

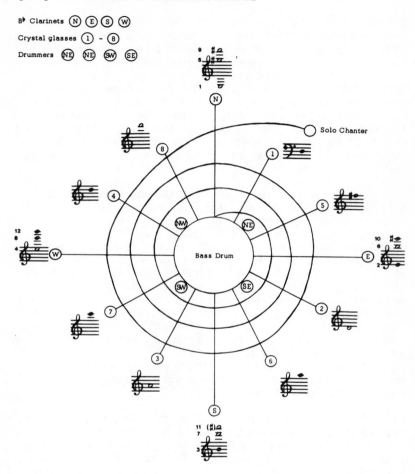

Mandala titled composition.   Copyright 1979 by Smith Publications.   Used by permission.

upon the fundamental D³, with the seventh and eleventh partials being in tune with the natural series.   The clarinets also use these pitches and perform long tones, changes in which are caused when the singer passes one of the spokes of the mandala.   The piece is about twenty to twenty-five minutes long and is easy for the audience to understand. The relationships among the structure of the mandala, the chanter's movements, and the harmonic changes of the drone

are obvious to anyone familiar with the overtone series.
The drumming meditation adds a crescendo from the beginning to the point where the soloist exits from the mandala.
The piece, which has been performed with Hebrew, Russian,
and Chinese texts, is similar to Meditation on the Points of
the Compass but is much simpler because the psychogram is
pared to the essentials of movement through the spiraling
overtones.

        In the pieces that have been discussed the mandala is
dynamic: its form and symbolism are the core of the composition.   In El Relicario de los Animales (1977), however,
Oliveros used a mandala in a different manner.   The staging
is a mandala pattern resembling a reliquary, which is like a
monstrance that is in the shape of a cross.   But the mandala's psychogram does not become sonic, and few people

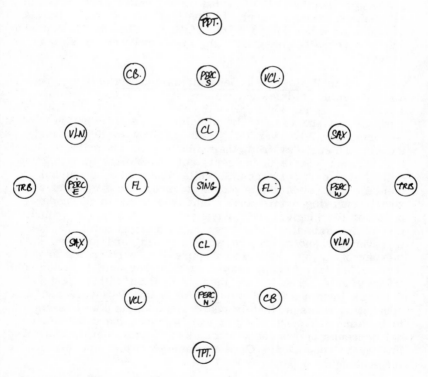

Mandala for El Relicario de los Animales.   Forthcoming
from Smith Publications.   Used by permission.

would perceive the meaning of the shape.   So instead of a
ceremony where the mandala is the structural basis, Oliveros used sonic imagination and the symbol of a reliquary
as the source of an improvisation.   Oliveros and Carol
Plantamura, for whom the piece was written, visited the
San Diego Zoo and selected four animals that would be contained in the reliquary of the piece.   They chose a tiger,
owl, wolf, and parrot.

The improvisation is divided into nine sections:
1) entrance--evocation, 2) tiger, 3) evocation, 4) owl,
5) evocation, 6) wolf, 7) evocation, 8) parrot, and 9) exit.
Eight guide words control the improvisation and are descriptions of musical situations: blend, echo, embellish,
extend, follow, free, lead, and silence.   Each word is carefully explained.   For example, embellish: "ornament any
stable, or weighted pitch, sound or rhythm of another player
with slides, shakes, turns, trills, fast figurations, vibratos,
tremolos or other forms of modulation.   The embellishment
may connect with, pass through, or extend what is embel-
lished."[10]

As in Willowbrook Generations and Reflections, performers must at times accurately imitate sounds, tempi,
dynamics, and rhythms.   But the new dimension in Oliveros's
work is that she is directly stimulating the imagination of the
performers.   Whenever the "lead" guide word is indicated,
the performers play from their imagination according to her
instructions.   Some instruments act as soloists imitating the
call of that particular animal while others are accompani-
mental.   One situation is quietly to make the sounds of a
small scurrying animal that might be moving in the under-
brush of the jungle.   The players are even told the symbolism of the animals.   The tiger represents hunger; the owl
is reverence and death; the wolf is mating and longing; and
the parrot is joy.   Oliveros requires the performers to put
themselves in a fantasy state in which they actually imagine
these sounds.   The person must hear them within, just as
Oliveros imagined her Variations or Sound Patterns, and the
connection between what is heard and what is played seems
to be almost a magical state that bypasses the usual musical concerns of reading pitches, keeping the tempo, and following the conductor.   Only extremely capable musicians have
the technique to perform El Relicario.

Oliveros has designed her directions so carefully that
a nonhierarchical relationship exists among all the musicians.

The singer stands on a red mound of earth in the center of the mandala and his or her sounds are more instrumental than vocal. At times the singer acts as a conductor, cueing ends of sections and signaling silence, but generally each musician is responsible for what he or she performs.

El Relicario may be difficult for an audience that does not want to accept animal-like sounds as part of music's domain. But animal sounds have always intrigued composers, especially the French. Jean Philippe Rameau's The Hen (1706?), Camille Saint-Saëns's Carnival of the Animals (1886), and Messiaen's Catalogue of the Birds (1956-58) come to mind. Today there are many animal-sound recordings available, such as whale songs, jungle environments, wolf songs, and John Lilly's work with dolphin communication.

El Relicario had a predecessor, To Those in the Grey Northwestern Rainforests (1976), in which one is to invent a forest creature and make sounds for that animal. Both pieces are in a compositional and performance mode that Oliveros has recently called "attentional states." The directions tune the performers' consciousness so that the desired sounds and forms are produced. These attentional states are directly concerned with the theory of sonic awareness and the essence of what it means to produce and shape sound.

By this time Oliveros was close to receiving her black belt in karate. The strict attention that she demands in these pieces parallels her own experiences with karate, which has not been easy for her. She failed and had to retake many of the tests, but she doggedly continues. Most of her attentional compositions are for highly proficient musicians and masters of their instruments, "black belt musicians."

The Witness (1979), which can be performed alone or with a partner, was commissioned by oboist Joseph Celli. The performer explores three attentional modes: imagined interior sounds, focused exterior sounds, and a combination of both interior and exterior modes. The performance directions are less strict than in El Relicario. For part one the performer must concentrate upon his or her imagined sounds, but the performed sounds must each be unique and unrelated to future sounds in the piece. The adjectives "unique" and "unrelated" are key words that cause a new

improvisational relationship to occur.   The performer ob-
serves his or her imagination, noticing and eliminating all
the recognized improvisational clichés and standard patterns
that come to mind, such as jazz riffs.   All formulae must
be discarded, and one must trust that the imagination will
produce fresh and new sounds.

The second attentional mode is different.   Instead of
interior sounds, the performer must now focus upon exterior
sounds, those made by the partner or imaginary partner.
One must respond immediately to the heard sounds.   The
kind of response is not specified.

In the last section the performers combine both the
interior and exterior modes of attention, including ambient
sounds, and the performer now becomes a third witness, an
outside observer of him- or herself in an all-embracing mode
spontaneously reacting to incoming information and observing
the results.   Since Oliveros always offers information about
and directions for her compositions in program notes or previous explanations to the audience, everyone knows that The
Witness is a testing situation.   A sloppy performance is in-
compatible with the milieu of the composition, and only performers who have a trust in themselves and personally know
what those years of practice have produced would put themselves in such a vulnerable situation.   It is an exciting test
for both audience and performer.   The piece speaks about a
harmony between the performer and the instrument.   Both
meet in the imagined sound.   In a performance by Celli and
the violinist Malcolm Goldstein one marveled at the breath
and bow control that both performers demonstrated.   The
oboe and string sounds were so timbrally complex that sometimes it was hard to distinguish between the two; multiphonics sounded like natural capabilities of the instruments, while
the traditionally clean, concise, and controlled oboe and
string timbres were out of place.   The sounds were those of
the moment, probably never again to be recreated exactly
the same way.

Double X (1979), another attentional piece, is for
eight paired players, each pair having like instruments and
all instruments having similar or overlapping range.   The
setup is a double X, another mandala figure, that surrounds
the audience.   The procedures that the players follow are
rather complicated, much like learning the rules of a new
game, but fundamentally easier than those in The Witness.
Pairs cue, attack tones together, which are then matched

by other pairs; intersect intervals at midpoints so that thirds are divided into seconds, octaves into tritones, etc.; and at times maintain silences that eliminate any opportunity for melodies or riffs to take place. The activities are like aural skills exercises. If unisons occur--an interesting possibility since pairs attack together but do not have prearranged pitches--then several other conditions eventuate. Judgments about pitch must constantly be made. The piece is divided into six rounds marked by the number of responses for each initiated sound, part one having two responses, part two having three responses, and so on. The result is a thickening texture that after the third round begins a retrograde action back to the conditions of round one. The last round is free. Cues may be initiated at random and answered by any two or more players. Like Willowbrook Generations and Reflections, Double X is a particularly helpful experience for young performers struggling to learn the value of ear-training.

Other attentional pieces by Oliveros are The Klickitat Ride for chorus and/or instruments (1979), Rock Piece for any number of performers (1979), and Traveling Companions for a percussion group (1980).

By 1980 Oliveros's directions to the performers had become sparse. In Anarchy Waltz (1980), which was included in a collaborative evening with Stuart Dempster and Robert Suderberg in a concert at the North Carolina School of the Arts, the directions are that each participant decides what Anarchy Waltz is. The primary concern is that the individual have the freedom he or she desires within the context of "the waltz."

The birth of Oliveros's niece, Daisy Pauline Oliveros, was an occasion for a beautiful attentional audience-participation piece, MMM, A Lullaby for Daisy Pauline (1980). The directions are for the audience to sound "MMM" by coloring the consonant M with different vowel sounds. The piece was performed at a national meeting of the Music Teachers' Association in Seattle, Washington, in the spring of 1980. Oliveros successfully engaged the entire audience, traditionally considered a conservative group of musicians, to perform her piece. Her technique is quietly to encourage members of the audience to pay attention to their breathing and then to begin to notice sounds in the room. Gradually they begin to form the MMM sounds, which Oliveros says is the sound of pleasure and joy. As sounds accumulate, more and more people participate, finding it satisfying both to produce the sounds and hear the results.

"MMM" also became the title for a recent paper and slide presentation, "Music, Meditation, and Mandala." Considering her work retrospectively, Oliveros realized that mandalas had shaped many of her pieces and noticed that the circuit diagrams she drew during her electronic-music days and her copious doodles produced on the back of faculty memoranda during committee meetings, were all mandalas. Some of the figurations later became pieces.   As part of her presentation she shows slides of these doodles and diagrams and then compares them to slides and tapes of the performances where the mandala shape can be seen and heard.

Notes

1.   José and Miriam Argüelles, Mandala (Berkeley, Calif.: Shambhala, 1972).

2.   Carl Sagan, Cosmos (New York: Random House, 1980).

3.   Argüelles, Mandala, p. 19.

4.   Margaret Porter's poem is included with the published score of Crow Two in Walter Zimmermann, editor, Desert Plants: Conversations with 23 American Musicians (Vancouver, B.C.:   Aesthetic Research Center), p. f.   Used by permission of the publisher.

5.   Oliveros discusses her feelings about audience reaction in Zimmermann's interview in Desert Plants, p. 167.

6.   One of Oliveros's statements in "Music, Meditation, and Mandala," soon to be published as part of her collected writings, Software for People, by Printed Editions, Barrytown, New York.

7.   For W. Y. Evans-Wentz's commentary on the sounds and purpose of Tibetan sacred music see W. Y. Evans-Wentz, The Tibetan Book of the Dead (London: Oxford University Press, 1960), pp. 128-129, footnote 4.

8.   For a discussion and a reproduction of the Yellow River Map see Richard Wilhem and Cary Baynes, translators, The I Ching (Princeton, N.J.:   Princeton University Press, 1967), p. 309.

9.   Pauline Oliveros, "The Yellow River Map," New Wilderness Letter, I, 3/4, 22-23.

10.   Pauline Oliveros, El Relicario de los Animales, p. 2 of the unpublished manuscript.   Used by permission.

9: EXPANSION

The mandala form that Oliveros has used in her later compositions is also a symbol of the way her career has expanded to include teaching, administration, writing, and lecturing.

Teaching was the first extension of her profession as a composer. Although never her main interest, Oliveros dedicated herself to teaching with the same exactitude as she gave to her composition. Like her music, her teaching methods were unconventional. One assignment was to investigate some aspect of world music. Instead of having a syllabus Oliveros conducted a fantasy exercise in which the students were to take an imaginary trip to a foreign country; the results of the exercise told them which music they were to study.

Oliveros related teaching to her research, at first featuring electronic-music technology and then, during the 1970s, using sonic meditation as aural exercises. Her karate study was reflected in a course on "Holism/Analysis," in which she used Ingber's analytical model of focal and global attention.

Listening, however, was always the focus of her teaching. She had general music students record sonic environments using a portable half-track monaural tape recorder. One student captured the groans and squeaks of a windmill; another recorded the envelope shapes of footsteps and conversations in a resonant stairwell; and many tapes featured ocean sounds.[1] Oliveros even arranged a fieldtrip to the San Diego Zoo so that the class could record the sounds of the animals during their early-morning feeding time.

[138]

Although Oliveros had many composition students, she did not teach theory or technique but rather suggested materials to stimulate ideas for pieces. Books about time, listening, ritual, performance art, psychology, and oriental philosophy were creative sources that she shared with students. Like her former teacher Erickson she insisted that students write with the intention of having their works performed. New students had to prove themselves by writing, copying, rehearsing, and performing a piece within the first quarter of study.

Oliveros found teaching, and such related activities as committee meetings, to be demanding, but she enjoyed her visiting professorships at York University (summer 1973) and Stanford University (fall 1978). Reduced academic responsibilities, however, were a welcome relief. During her semester at Stanford Oliveros relaized that she should resign from university teaching before she was completely consumed by administrative duties.

Also, as her creative reputation grew, so did her professional responsibilities. As mentioned before, Oliveros was a member of the composers/librettist panel for the National Endowment for the Arts (1976-79) and a member of New York State's Creative Arts Public Service (1977-78). She served on the boards of the Composers' Forum, Meet the Composers, the Journal of Social and Theoretical Biology, the Samaya Foundation (a society for preservation of Tibetan art), and the Physical Studies Institute, as well as being a contributing editor for The New Wilderness Letter. It became apparent that she had to make a choice between continuing these professional administrative activities or returning to a simpler life, one in which she would have time for her own creative work.

Oliveros decided to give up teaching. In August 1981 she moved to Mount Tremper, New York, a secluded area of the Catskills, where she now lives in an A-frame cabin. Although her A-frame does not have running water, it is equipped with a computer. Alvin Toffler's "electronic cottage" of the future is even more appropriate than Toffler himself described in his The Third Wave. [2] Oliveros uses the computer to edit her compositions, organize her secretarial and managerial work, and keep financial records. One wonders if the computer will affect her future compositions. [3]

One of the reasons Oliveros left the university was

that she would be freer to travel. Her new location is
close enough to New York City to allow her to collaborate
and participate in new-music concerts. Also, she would
now have the time to accept the increasing number of concerts and speaking engagements.

One engagement in the spring of 1980 was the performance of her Ceremony of Sounds (1974) by a radio station in Columbia, Missouri. The radio listeners were asked
to be aware of sounds that were single and indivisible, and
then they were to call the radio station and someone would
come to record the sound. Ed Herrmann, program director
for station KOPN-FM, reported that the community response
was enthusiastic. One person even wanted a certain motor-
cycle sound to be part of the performance. Oliveros edited
the final taped version, and the piece was aired on one of
Herrmann's new-music programs, "Ionizations."

In Ceremony of Sounds the listener becomes both composer and performer by selecting the material for the piece.
In another work, Cheap Commissions (1976), Oliveros performs the act of composing for anyone who wants to buy a
piece. For several years she received commissions through
the mail. One woman sent a dollar and wanted an original
piece of art for her husband. Oliveros answered each re-
quest with a personal letter and composition, even though she
did not know some of the people. Generally the piece she
composed was a simple instruction that made the recipient
aware of sound. For example: Fill a glass with water and
take it to a sunny window. Observe the effects of the light
on the water and imagine sound to accompany this phenomenon. Part of Oliveros's farewell to the West Coast was a
performance of Cheap Commissions at a flea market in Leucadia. When requested to write a Cheap Commission for
this book (the commission will be one percent of the first
royalty check) her reply was a variation of her flea-market
experience: "Make a collection of the cheapest sounds you
know. Set up a booth at a flea market and sell them for as
much as possible."

Both Ceremony of Sounds and Cheap Commissions
were influenced by Oliveros's interest in performance art.
Several of her artist friends have been active in creating a
synthesis among the plastic and performance arts. Eleanor
Antin, who is on the faculty of the University of California
at San Diego, used Oliveros's house and grounds for one of
her pieces, "Angels of Mercy,"[4] and Oliveros's notebooks

contain several references to Antin's 100 Boots, a serialized performance in which photographs of boots are sent through the mail. Oliveros's Post Card Theater (1972) used the postal system as the performance medium. She bought one hundred postcards of St. Francis of Assisi in memory of her days in San Francisco and wrote the following dream image on each card: "I saw an elephant walking on the water." She addressed the cards to herself, mailed them from different locations, and kept careful records about where they were mailed and when she received them.

In 1975 Oliveros began a performance series called Theater of Substitution. She had herself photographed as different persons--a Spanish señora, a suburban housewife dressed in a polyester-knit pant suit, and a lethargic-looking professor clad in an academic robe. For one performance Jackson MacLow agreed to be Oliveros and took her place at the New York Philharmonic's "A Celebration of Women Composers" concert on November 10, 1975. Jackson wrote about his experience in his article "being Pauline   narrative of a substitution" in Big Deal, Fall 1976. Oliveros has reversed the roles and been Jackson. 5

As we have seen, the titles of several pieces by Oliveros refer to Linda Montano (as Rose Mountain), but Montano's own work as a visual artist doing performance pieces in museums, galleries, cafeterias, and other public places has affected Oliveros. Many of Montano's pieces are autobiographical and are documented in her Art in Everyday Life. 6 Frequently Montano and Oliveros perform in each other's compositions; Montano has even made a videotape of Oliveros's work.

In August 1981 Montano and Oliveros collaborated on a piece called Monkey, which was premiered during Oliveros's residency at the Cabrillo Music Festival. Monkey was performed by thirty children, ten and eleven years of age, from the Freedom Elementary School in Aptos. Montano guided the children in creating the narrative, which is an allegory about monkeys who live in a quasihuman world. Oliveros's guidance is evident in certain images that the children used, such as large circles, a wise old crow, and a ritual snake dance.

The program on which Monkey appeared was partially funded by a grant from the BankAmerica Foundation and the National Endowment for the Arts. It featured a performance

of Oliveros's <u>Angels and Demons</u> (1980), in which the audience (including the children) was invited to participate.   The
instructions were:

> Angels are protectors and guardians.   In this
> piece, angels are represented by those who blend
> as perfectly as possible with long, steady tones
> with the ensemble on stage and those around them-
> selves.   Demons are the spirits of creative genius.
> In this piece, demons are represented by those who
> listen carefully to their own imagination and offer
> unique sounds which are guided by their own demon.
>   You are invited to join the piece by becom-
> ing an angel or demon.   Angels may change into
> demons or demons to angels during the course of
> the meditation. [7]

There were mixed reviews about the Cabrillo Festival
performance of <u>Monkey</u> and <u>Angels and Demons</u>.   Richard
Pontzious of the <u>San Francisco Examiner</u> disliked both pieces
and titled his August 29, 1981, review "Even the Participants
Hated It." But on August 28, 1981, Charles Shere of the
Oakland <u>Tribune</u> wrote that Oliveros "had charmed the children, but had also tapped their ancient creative energy and
intuitive sense of analogy and symbolism."

Earlier in the year Mark Swed of the <u>Los Angeles
Herald Examiner</u> had been impressed by a performance of
<u>Angels and Demons</u> at a California Women Composers Con-
cert held at the Woman's Building in Los Angeles.   On
April 13, 1981, he wrote:

> The composer, who sat on the stage with eyes
> closed, displaying a concentration so intense it
> was almost palpable and certainly contagious, in-
> vited the audience to join her and the instrumen-
> talist in an euphonious drone designed to excite
> the imagination to produce unique sounds.   Friday
> night the pull between the collective consonance
> and disruptive solo improvisations resulted in a
> magnificent musical drama.
>   The most startling aspect of this supposedly
> unpredictable piece was its resulting musical form,
> with its sense of controlled tension-and-release as
> well as the mysterious feeling of finality....

Since the late 1970s Oliveros's titles and images have

become overtly spiritual; examples are <u>Angels and Demons</u> and <u>The Witness</u>. Although she has a professed interest in Tibetan Buddhism, Oliveros refuses to become a devotee of any sect. She attends some Tibetan services and teachings but insists upon her own style of living and practicing spiritual beliefs.

<u>Tashi Gomang</u> (1981), a large orchestral work premiered at the Cabrillo Music Festival, is an example of a piece that has a mixture of spiritual influences: Tibetan Buddhism, Yoga's seven chakras, and <u>I Ching</u> imagery. The title is Tibetan and means "good flying," in the sense of having a successful meditation. The musicians' meditation is trying to hear and perform a sonic mandala, the first sixty-four harmonic overtones that are present in the contrabass's E string.

The orchestra is divided into four groups of fourteen performers, as shown in the diagram on page 144. The butterfly shape of this seating arrangement is another symbol of good flying.

Oliveros returned to a strict control of time for <u>Tashi Gomang</u>. It is twenty-eight minutes long and divided into seven four-minute sections. These sections correspond to Yoga's seven chakras, a symbolic system of the human body's energy centers pictured as emanating from the base of the spine and rising to the tip of the head. A particular color is associated with each chakra: red, orange, yellow, green, blue, violet, and white. <u>Tashi Gomang</u> is accompanied by a lighting scheme using this color progression. An informed listener will recognize the progression and its relationship to the chakras, and the meditating musicians should be influenced by these structural color changes.

Each of these chakra sections is further divided into four parts that are dominated by imagery from the <u>I Ching</u>. When composing the piece, Oliveros tossed coins for <u>I Ching</u> readings and used the resulting hexagrams to determine the images (thunder, wind, earth, fire, lake, water, mountain, and heaven) and pitches for each part. The configuration of the yin and yang lines together with the changing lines specified which odd and/or even overtones should be used.

<u>Tashi Gomang</u> is extremely complex because the performers must listen for specific pitches, which are often microtones, and then determine if those pitches are repro-

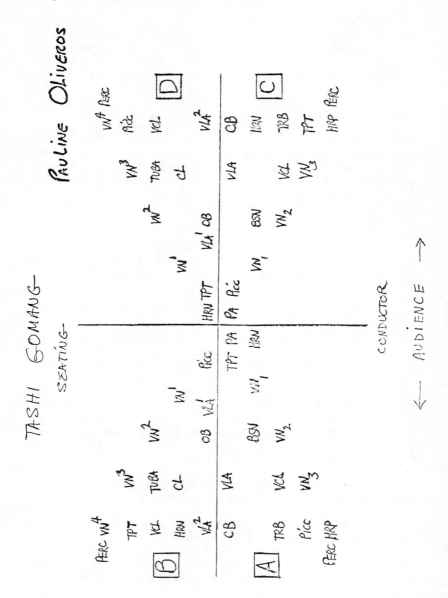

Seating diagram for Tashi Gomang. Forthcoming from Smith Publications. Used by permission.

ducible on their instruments. (The piano does not have to be tuned to agree with the natural harmonic system because Oliveros instructs the performers to omit pitches that are not present on their instruments.) Also, each image has specific instructions.   For instance, the first image of distant thunder has a dynamic marking of pp-mp.   An accompanying graphic (see Example 16) shows thunder's jagged sonic wave lengths, and the musicians are given the following directions: "Simulate the sound of thunder by using a thunder-like dynamic shape for your passage.   Pitches may be used in any order and repeated.   Blend carefully with the percussionist who initiates the thunder and with the other members of your group. "

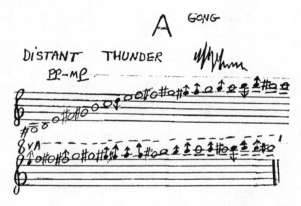

Example 16.   Partial series and graphic used in the Distant Thunder image in section I of Tashi Gomang.   Forthcoming from Smith Publications.   Used by permission.

As in El Relicario de los Animales, Oliveros controls the improvisation and is specific about how the image should affect the sound.   Tashi Gomang, however, is even more difficult because only certain pitches may be used and the performers must know what they are going to do.   Each part is only one minute long, so there is no time to experiment.   In addition the individual's sound must also blend with what his or her group is doing because the group is responsible for creating only one composite image, not a collection of solo images as in El Relicario.

The other images used in Tashi Gomang have similar specifications and graphics.   Some images are repeated (such

as mountain and howling wind), and, although the graphics
and directions are the same, the pitches are different so
that the image sounds both the same and different.

When a group is not performing its image (each group
has one image per section), then the participants play a harmony, which Oliveros calls the source.   It changes halfway
through each section.   The I Ching readings determined both
the source's pitch content and the specific collection of the
E harmonic series.   Oliveros's direction for the source is:
"Play the missing pitch."   The performers have to listen
carefully and then try to supply the sound of the notated
pitches that they are not hearing.

Although Tashi Gomang resembles other texture- and
timbre-oriented music in the style of György Ligeti or
Krzysztof Penderecki, the presence of this continuous E-
drone and its harmonic overtones adds a resonance to the
sound that one does not often hear.   The listener perceives
a steady calm that is surrounded by an active mixture of
changing images and textures and is simultaneously aware
of both the whole and its parts.

Oliveros continues to collaborate with other artists.
In the fall of 1981 she provided the music for six performances in New York City of Merce Cunningham's dance
Events.   With Malcolm Goldstein and David Tudor she performed The Witness for several evenings, but she also designed a new composition for the occasion.   She had a postcard of a lake bearing the inscription CHARGOGGAGOGG-
MANCHAUGGAGOGGCHAUBUNABUNBAGAUGG, which means,
"You fish on your side, I will fish on my side, and no one
will fish in the middle."   Oliveros liked both the lake image
and the onomatopoeia of the inscription and decided to use
the postcard as the score for an improvisation.   Karl Berger, Jackson MacLow, Guy Klucevsek, and Oliveros performed the piece, which turned out to have a synchronous
overtone because, unbeknown to Oliveros, MacLow had a
copy of the same postcard displayed on the wall near his
desk.

These coincidences are common occurrences for
Oliveros.   Her career has been a series of transformations
that at first seem incongruous but later follow a logical development.   Her early work with electronic music eventually evolved into consciousness studies, and her theater pieces
became visual and sonic mandalas.   But all of her efforts

have columinated in sonic meditation, which can best be understood as improvisation guided by meditation.   Oliveros has followed this direction since 1970.   It represents the maturing of her musical style.

Like John Cage she has confronted the manner of hearing and performing in American culture.   Oliveros certainly has been influenced by Cage, and although they share an interest in the material aspects of sound, Oliveros's ideas about composition are quite different.   Her manner of writing is personal and controlled whereas Cage's is impersonal and determined by chance operations.   Frequently Oliveros's presence is an important aspect of her work, especially when it includes audience participation.   Her body language of sitting cross-legged on a stage or in the center of a circle with house lights dimmed communicates her attitudes about sound and performing.   Probably the most striking element that Cage and Oliveros have in common is their strong personalities.   Their artwork is either accepted or rejected but cannot be passively received or ignored.

Oliveros can also be compared with Charles Ives (1874-1954).   Both share spiritual characteristics.   Ives's transcendental philosophy is apparent in the titles and musical quotations that he used, whereas Oliveros's naturalistic and quasi-Taoist-Buddhist philosophy is the basis of the way she hears and uses sound.   Although her spiritualism is a merging of Eastern and Western cultures, it is an American expression of the struggle for freedom.   Ives sought to develop a new attitude toward musical material, superimposing hymn tunes on other textures, rhythms, and musical ideas.   Oliveros promotes a musical democracy in which the barriers among composers, performers, and audience are broken down.   But, unlike Ives, she has not been isolated. Oliveros has been active in groups: the San Francisco Tape Music Center, the university community, performance galleries, and collaborations with other artists.   Her works are performed soon after they are composed and are noticed by the press.

Probably Oliveros has more in common with Harry Partch (1901-1974).   Like Partch she is concerned about tuning and uses it as a metaphor for all of her work with global and focal attention.   Partch said that he went outside of music, being influenced by Chinese lullabies, Yaqui Indian songs, and Greek drama.   He abandoned European concert tradition and wrote what he called "corporeal music," often associating music with myth and requiring musicians to learn new performance skills, acting abilities, and vocal fluency with microtonal materials.   His ideas demanded that he build instruments to realize the kinds of sounds that he was hearing.   Oliveros has not been an instrument maker, except for her work with tape-delay setups, but her music is corporeal in the sense that she uses the voice, cere- monies, and at times the acting capabilities of performers. Partch always wrote for highly specialized musicians, peo- ple whom he himself trained, and designed his own notation for his complex scores.   Oliveros, on the other hand, writes for a large gamut of performers, and improvisation is almost always the source of her pieces.   Partch was able to perform what he wrote; composing was not an ab- straction or the most important aspect of his work.   Mak- ing sounds was his goal.   The same is true of Oliveros.

In addition to reflecting many of the major develop- ments in new music, Oliveros's career adds such extramu- sical influences as visual imagery, theater, performance art, martial arts, and meditation.   But Pauline Olveros's music remains an enigma.   There is no doubt that her compositions are feminist statements about artistic free- dom and self-expression.   Although it is difficult to fore- cast if others will continue her daring approach to art, it is hoped that her emphasis of carefully listening to sound will be perpetuated.

Notes

1.   Oliveros discussed some of these innovative teaching techniques when she was a member of the 1968 International Music Congress's forum "The Sounds of Things to Come." For a transcription of what was said see "International Mu- sic Congress: Forum (The Sounds of Things to Come)," Music and Artists, 2 (1969), 23.   Notice Aaron Cop- land's embarrassing moments when he realized that Oliveros was the only woman composer on the panel.

2.   Alvin Toffler, The Third Wave (New York: William Morrow, 1980).

3.   Previously she had used the computer to catalog her musical and written works and published the collection as Software for People, a title using computer-language imagery.

The book is available through Printed Editions, a cooperative press that has evolved from Dick Higgins's Something Else Press (founded in 1964), which published works by John Cage, Higgins, and Alison Knowles.   Also available from Printed Editions is Pauline's Proverbs/Compiled by "Rosita"/Christmas 1976, a small volume containing Oliveros's homely maxims about succeeding in life.

4.   Eleanor Antin's "Angel of Mercy" is documented in the exhibition booklet for the La Jolla Museum of Contemporary Art showing, from September 10-October 23, 1977.

5.   Oliveros's article "Being Jackson" is published in Paper Air, II, 3, 34-35.

6.   Linda Montano, Art in Everyday Life (Barrytown, N.Y.: Printed Editions, 1981).

7.   The score for Angels and Demons was printed in the program notes for the Cabrillo Music Festival, August 27, 1981.   Used by permission of the composer.

AFTERWORD

> The most important thing about composing is
> one's motivation. I wish for my work to be
> beneficial to myself and to all who experience it.

Pauline Oliveros

CHRONOLOGY

1932   Pauline Oliveros born in Houston, Texas, May 30.

1945   Studies accordion with Willard Palmer.

1949   Enrolls at the University of Houston.

1950   Studies French horn with Bernard Valkenier.

1951   Studies composition with Paul Keopke at the University of Houston.

1952   Performances of Song for Piano and Song for Horn and Harp and Dance Band at the University of Houston. Moves to San Francisco.

1953   Studies composition with Robert Erickson.

1954   Studies French horn with Earl Saxton.

1957   Graduates from San Francisco State College and receives Mu Phi Alumnae Scholarship. Begins work with group improvisation. Three Songs for Soprano and Piano.

1960   Variations for Sextet. Starts Sonics group in collaboration with Ramon Sender.

1961   Receives Pacifica Foundation Award for Variations for Sextet. Time Perspectives, Trio for Flute, Piano and Page Turner, and Sound Patterns. Joins Morton Subotnick and Ramon Sender at San Francisco Tape Music Center.

1962   Receives Foundation Gaudeamus prize in Holland for Best Foreign Work. Travels to Holland, Sweden, Germany, and France.

[152]

1963   Outline for Flute, Percussion and String Bass.   San
Francisco Tape Music Center moves to Divisadero
Street and establishes concert series.

1964   Begins developing interest in theatrical and visual
materials.   Organizes Tudor Fest and premieres
Duo for Accordion and Bandoneon with Possible
Mynah Bird Obligato [sic], See Saw Version in col-
laboration with Elizabeth Harris at San Francisco
Tape Music Center.

1965   Premieres Pieces of Eight at University of Arizona.
Bye Bye Butterfly.

1966   Studies briefly with Hugh Le Caine at University of
Toronto and composes I of IV.   Collaborates with
Elizabeth Harris for Theater Piece for Trombone
Player.   Appointed director of Mills Tape Music
Center.

1967   Premieres Circuitry for Percussion at Mills College.   Appointed to faculty of University of California, San Diego.

1968   Double Basses at Twenty Paces.   Performs Some
Sound Observations with Amplified Manhattan at
Electric Circus in New York City.   Composes
Valentine for Sonic Arts Group.

1969   Collaborates with Merce Cunningham for In Memoriam Nikola Tesla: Cosmic Engineer (Canfield).
Aeolian Partitions commissioned by Aeolian Players.

1970   Music for Expo '70 performed at World's Fair in
Osaka, Japan.   Premieres Meditation on the Points
of the Compass at Wesleyan University, Blooming-
ton, Illinois.   Premieres To Valerie Solanas and
Marilyn Monroe in Recognition of Their Desperation
---- at Hope College, Holland, Michigan.   Begins
exploring ritual and ceremony and looking for ways
of composing for despecialized performers.   Forms
♀ Ensemble.   Writes article "And Don't Call Them
Lady Composers" for New York Times.

1971   Sonic Meditations I-XII.   Link commissioned by
Larry Livingston for Palomar College, Oceanside,
California.

1972   Begins karate lessons with Lester Ingber.   Per-
       forms Sonic Images at California State College, Los
       Angeles.

1973   Visiting Professor at York University, Toronto.
       Appointed Faculty Fellow at Center for Music Ex-
       periment.   Sonic Meditations XII-XXV.   Awarded
       Guggenheim fellowship.

1974   Participates in Meta Music Festival in Berlin.   Pre-
       mieres Crow, commissioned by Creative Associates
       at Center for Creative and Performing Arts, State
       University of New York, Buffalo, and premieres at
       Albright-Knox Gallery in Buffalo.   Appointed to the
       composer/librettist panel of National Endowment for
       the Arts.

1975   Premieres A Ceremony of Sounds, composed for
       Tamar Reed at University of North Dakota.   Or-
       ganizes Mandeville Opening Festival and premieres
       Crow Two at University of California, San Diego.

1976   Premieres Willowbrook Generations and Reflections,
       commissioned by Donald La Roche for Willowbrook
       High School Band.   Appointed director of Center for
       Music Experiment.

1977   Rose Moon commissioned by Wesleyan University,
       Middletown, Connecticut.   Awarded Beethoven Prize
       by city of Bonn for Bonn Feier.   Premieres The
       Yellow River Map in collaboration with Al Chung
       Liang Huang.   King Kong Sing Along performed at
       Annual Festival of the Avant Garde, World Trade
       Center, New York City.

1978   ✺ commissioned by Independent Composers' Asso-
       ciation, Los Angeles.   Visiting Professor at Stan-
       ford University.

1979   Premieres El Relicario de los Animales during
       Contemporary Music Festival at California Institute
       for the Arts.   Premieres Double X and Rock Piece
       at Lenox Arts Center, Lenox, Massachusetts.   Com-
       poses The Witness, commissioned by Joseph Celli.

1980   Premieres Crow's Nest in collaboration with Elaine
       Summers at Guggenheim Museum in New York City.

Performs MMM, A Lullaby for Daisy Pauline at
Walker Arts Center, Minneapolis. Receives black
belt in Shotokan-style karate. Participates in College Music Society Improvisation Project at Banff,
Alberta. Participates in Women and Music Festival
in Bonn, Germany.

1981   Premieres Tashi Gomang and Monkey at Cabrillo
Festival and Traveling Companions at University of
California, San Diego. Moves to Mount Tremper,
New York.

CATALOG OF COMPOSITIONS

Compositions for piano

1951   Ode to a Morbid Marble
        Piano solo
        Manuscript

1952   Song for Piano
        Piano solo
        Manuscript
        Premiered May 25, 1952, University
        of Houston

1953   Fugue for Piano
        Piano solo
        Manuscript
        Premiered May 12, 1955, Composers
        Workshop, San Francisco State
        College

1954   Essay for Piano
        Piano solo
        Manuscript
        Premiered May 12, 1955, Composers
        Workshop, San Francisco State
        College

Compositions for accordion

1957   Concert Piece for Accordion
        Accordion solo
        Manuscript
        Premiered 1957, Composers Workshop,
        San Francisco State College

1959   Eighteen Children's Pieces for Accordion

Accordion solo
Manuscript

1965   Duo for Accordion and Bandoneon with
Possible Mynah Bird Obligato [sic],
Seesaw Version
Accordion, bandoneon, seesaw, bird
cage, and mynah bird
Manuscript
Premiered March 1964, San Francisco
Tape Music Center
Commissioned by David Tudor

1966   Accordion
Amplified accordion with tape-delay
system and eight channels
Manuscript

Vocal compositions

1957   Three Songs for Soprano and Horn
Texts by Carl Sandburg and Walt
Whitman
Soprano and French horn
Manuscript
Premiered November 18, 1957, Com-
posers Workshop, San Francisco
State College

Three Songs for Soprano and Piano
Texts by Robert Duncan and Charles
Olson
Soprano and piano
Published by Smith Publications, 1976
Premiered November 18, 1957, Com-
posers Workshop, San Francisco
State College

1961   Sound Patterns
Mixed chorus
Published by Edition Tonos, 1964
Premiered September 10, 1962,
Gaudeamus International Music
Week
Reviewed by J. Geraedts, "Internation-
ale muziekweek 1962 'Gaudeamus,'"

Mens en Mel, October 1962, pp. 296-299; Alfred Frankenstein, "Extended Voices," High Fidelity, March 1965, p. 110; Eric Salzman, "Musicotechnology: The Medium Is the Music," Hi Fi/Stereo Review, May 1968, p. 98; and Eric Salzman, "Record Reviews," Stereo Review, August 1971, p. 89

1968   O Ha Ah
Mixed chorus
Manuscript
Premiered Smith College, Northampton, Massachusetts

Compositions for small chamber ensembles

1951   Undertone
Violin and piano
Manuscript
Premiered May 25, 1952, University of Houston

1952   Song for Horn and Harp and Dance Band
Manuscript
Premiered May 20, 1952, University of Houston
Reviewed by Don Barthelme, "University Lyric Festival Gets a Lively Start," Houston Post, May 21, 1952

1953   Prelude and Fugue
String quartet
Manuscript
Premiered May 18, 1954, Composers Workshop, San Francisco State College

1955   Trio for Clarinet, Horn and Bassoon
Manuscript
Premiered May 12, 1955, Composers Workshop, San Francisco State College

1956   Serenade for Viola and Bassoon
Manuscript

Premiered May 13, 1957, Composers
Workshop, San Francisco State
College

1960   Variations for Sextet
Flute, clarinet, trumpet, French horn,
cello, and piano
Published by Smith Publications, 1974
Premiered April 20, 1960, San Fran-
cisco Conservatory of Music
Reviewed by Alfred Frankenstein,
"Modern Music Festival Opens,"
San Francisco Chronicle, April 21,
1960; Alexander Fried, "Music by
Modern Composers: Oliveros Work
Is Impressive," San Francisco Ex-
aminer, April 21, 1960; Arthur
Bloomfield, "A Star Is Born," Mu-
sical America, March 1962, p. 14;
Bertram Levy, "Urbana: Report
from the University of Illinois,"
Perspectives of New Music, IV, 2
(1966), 181-183; and Richard Pont-
zious, "Cabrillo Festival's New
Perspectives," San Francisco Ex-
aminer, August 21, 1981

1961   Trio for Flute, Piano and Page Turner
Published by Smith Publications, 1977
Premiered 1961, Composers Forum,
San Francisco Museum of Art
Reviewed by Udo Kasemets, "Current
Chronicle," Musical Quarterly,
1964, p. 518; and Bertram Levy,
"Urbana: Report from the Univer-
sity of Illinois," Perspectives of
New Music, IV, 2 (1966), 181-183.

Trio for Accordion, Trumpet, and String
Bass
Published by Smith Publications, 1981
Premiered August 1964, New Hamp-
shire Music Festival

1000 Acres
String quartet
Manuscript

Music for dancers

1964   **Fifteen for Four Dancers**
Improvisation
Manuscript

Five for Trumpet and Dancer
Manuscript
Premiered winter 1964, television
    station KQED, San Francisco

Seven Passages for Elizabeth Harris
Two-channel tape
Premiered winter 1963, Marines
    Memorial Theater, San Francisco

1965   **Before the Music Ends**
Dance theater choreography by
    Elizabeth Harris
Two-channel tape
Premiered November 1965, San
    Francisco State College

1966   **The Bath**
Dancers and tape-delay system
Premiered October 1966, San Fran-
    cisco Tape Music Center
Commissioned by Ann Halprin

1969   **In Memoriam Nikola Tesla, Cosmic Engineer**
Live electronics
Premiered during March 1969 tour of
    Cunningham Dance Company
Commissioned by Merce Cunningham
    Foundation for "Canfield"

Music for films and plays

1958   **Cock a Doodle Dandy**, incidental music
    for play
Accordion
Manuscript
Premiered spring 1958, Marines
    Memorial Theater, San Francisco
Commissioned by Herbert Blau for
    Actors' Workshop

4H Club, music for film documentary
    Clarinet, flute, guitar, and double bass
    Manuscript

Tom Sawyer, incidental music for play
    Manuscript

View from the Bridge, incidental music
    for play
    Violin, flute mandolin, guitar, accor-
       dion, double bass, and two percus-
       sionists
    Manuscript

1962   Lulu, incidental music for play
    Prepared piano and flute
    Manuscript
    Premiered spring 1962, San Francisco
       Poetry Center Festival, San Fran-
       cisco Museum of Art
    Commissioned by Leonard Woolf

1963   Art in Woodcut, music for film
    Manuscript
    Commissioned by filmmaker Proctor
       Jones

1965   Candelaio, music for San Francisco
    Mime Troupe
    Vocal
    Manuscript
    Premiered summer 1965, Sausalito,
       California
    Commissioned by R. G. Davis

Cat O' Nine Tails, for theater group
    Two-channel tape
    Premiered July 1965, Walker Art
       Center, Minneapolis

Covenant, music for film
    Two-channel tape of live improvisation
       recorded for film

The Chronicles of Hell, music for San
    Francisco Mime Troupe
    Two-channel tape
    Premiered during San Francisco Mime

Troupe's 1965 winter tour
Commissioned by R. G. Davis

The Exception and the Rule, music for
San Francisco Mime Troupe
Environmental sound sources
Premiered spring 1965, San Francisco
Commissioned by R. G. Davis

1967   Lysistrata, music for play
Two-channel tape
Premiered April 1967, Mills College,
Oakland

1969   Events, music for film by Lynn Lonidier
Live soundtrack using cello, voices,
other instruments, and audience
participation
Reviewed by Stephanie Miller, "Oliveros in Exciting Concert," Seattle
Post-Intelligence, October 15, 1970

1976   Twenty-two Cuts from the Red Horse----,
music for Mabou Mines experimental
theater group directed by Lee Breuer
Manuscript

Electronic music

1961   Time Perspectives
Four-channel tape
Premiered December 18, 1961, San
Francisco Conservatory of Music

1964   Apple Box
Amplified apple box and small objects
Premiered August 1964, Center Harbor,
New Hampshire

Apple Box Orchestra
Amplified apple box, mallets, and
small sound producers
Premiered January 1965, Encore
Theater, San Francisco

1965   Bye Bye Butterfly
Two-channel tape

Recorded by 1750 Arch, "New Music
for Electronic and Recorded Media,"
S-1765
Reviewed by John Rockwell, "Which
Works of the 70's Were Significant?,"
New York Times, July 27, 1980

Mnemonics II
Two-channel tape

Mnemonics III
Two-channel tape

Mnemonics V
Two-channel tape
Premiered January 1965, Encore
Theater, San Francisco

Rock Symphony
Live electronics and tape delay
Premiered January 1965, Encore
Theater, San Francisco

1966   Big Mother Is Watching You
Two-channel tape
Tape is available from Smith Publica-
tions, 1978
Premiered July 22, 1967, Tapeathon,
San Francisco

5000 Miles
Two-channel tape
Premiered July 22, 1967, Tapeathon,
San Francisco

Jar Piece
Two-channel tape
Recorded by Marathon Music Incor-
porated and tape is available from
Smith Publications, 1978

NO MO
Two-channel tape

I of IV
Two-channel tape
Recorded by Odyssey, "Music of Our
Time," 32 16 0160

Reviewed by Alfred Frankenstein,
"Electronic Music--Masterpieces
and Other Pieces (recording),"
High Fidelity/Musical America,
February 1968, p. 45.

II of IV
Two-channel tape
Tape is available from Smith Publica-
tions, 1978
Premiered July 22, 1967, Tapeathon,
San Francisco

The Day I Disconnected the Erase Head
and Forgot to Reconnect It
Two-channel tape
Tape is available from Smith Publica-
tions, 1978
Premiered July 22, 1967, Tapeathon,
San Francisco

Ultra Sonic Studies in Real Time
Two-channel tape

1967   Alien Bog
Two-channel tape
Tape is available from Smith Publica-
tions, 1978
Premiered July 22, 1967, Tapeathon,
San Francisco

Beautiful Soop
Two-channel tape
Tape is available from Smith Publica-
tions, 1978
Premiered July 22, 1967, Tapeathon,
San Francisco
Reviewed by Theodore Strongin, "Mu-
sic and Theater Share Same Circuit
at Electric Circus," New York
Times, July 10, 1968

Bog Bog
Two-channel tape

Bog Road with Bird Call Patch
Two-channel tape

Premiered October 7, 1970, Hope
College, Holland, Michigan

Circuitry for Percussion and Light
Premiered June 1967 at Mills College,
Oakland

Engineers Delight
Piccolo, seven conductors (not electronic) for amplification of program
sources, four turntables, and modulation
Premiered February 1967, University
of Illinois, Urbana

Mills Bog
Two-channel tape
Premiered July 22, 1967, Tapeathon,
San Francisco

1968   Some Sound Observations
Two-channel tape
Reviewed by Theodore Strongin, "Mu-
sic and Theater Share Same Circuit
at Electric Circus," New York
Times, July 10, 1978

1970   Music for Expo '70
Multichannel tape
Premiered April 14, 1970, World's
Fair in Osaka, Japan

Theater pieces

1964   Pieces of Eight
Flute, oboe, French horn, contra-
bassoon, bass clarinet, trumpet,
trombone, clarinet, and conductor
Published by Smith Publications, 1977
Premiered March 1965, University of
Arizona, Tucson
Reviewed by Arthur Bloomfield, "Lud-
wig Frowns: Far Out on Divisa-
dero," San Francisco Examiner,
May 4, 1965
Commissioned by Barney Childs

1965   A Theater Piece
       Fifteen actors, film, projections,
           players, and two-channel tape
       Manuscript
       Premiered November 1965 at Encore
           Theater with San Francisco Mime
           Troupe

       George Washington Slept Here
       Amplified violin, film, projections,
           and two-channel tape
       Manuscript
       Premiered November 10, 1965, San
           Francisco Tape Music Center

       George Washington Slept Here Too
       Four performers, one grand piano,
           one toy Sonic Blaster by Mattel or
           one real pistol with blank, and one
           slide projector
       Score published in Soundings, January
           1972, p. 9

       I've Got You Under My Skin
       Solo percussionist and Bat Man
       Manuscript

       Light Piece for David Tudor
       Electronically modified piano, lights,
           film, and four-channel tape
       Manuscript
       Premiered November 10, 1965, San
           Francisco Tape Music Center
       Commissioned by David Tudor

1966   Hallo
       Electronically modified piano, two
           tape-delay systems, violins, voice,
           actor, light projections, and
           dancers
       Manuscript
       Premiered October 31, 1966, for
           opening of Mills Tape Music Cen-
           ter at Mills College, Oakland

       Participle Dangling in Honor of Gertrude
       Stein
       Mobile, film, and two-channel tape

Manuscript
Premiered winter 1967, Minneapolis

Theater Piece for Trombone Player
Trombone, hoses, candles, and two-
channel tape
Choreography by Elizabeth Harris
Forthcoming from Smith Publications
Premiered March 11, 1966, San
Francisco Tape Music Center
Reviewed by Robert Commanday, "An
Adventurous Trombone Man," San
Francisco Chronicle, May 24, 1967;
Theodore Strongin, "Concert Is
Given For the Fun of It," New York
Times, March 27, 1968; and Con-
rad Susa, "Foss: Evenings of New
Music," High Fidelity/Musical
America, June 1968, MA pp. 16-17.
Commissioned by Stuart Dempster

1968   Double Basses at Twenty Paces
Two referees, two bassists, and a
conductor
Published by Smith Publications, 1978
Premiered February 11, 1969, Uni-
versity of California, San Diego
Reviewed by Andrew De Rhen, "Inter-
media Institute," High Fidelity/
Musical America, January 1972,
MA p. 20.

Evidence for Competing Bimolecular and
Termolecular Mechanisms in the Hy-
drochlorination of Cyclohexine
Modular theater piece for specialized
and unspecialized performers
Manuscript
Premiered January 1968, University
of California, San Diego

Festival House
Orchestra, chorus, mimes, films,
and projections
Manuscript
Premiered July 1968, New Hampshire
Music Festival, Chocorua

Night Jar
    Viola d'amore, tape, film, and mime
    Manuscript
    Premiered July 8, 1968, Electric
        Circus, New York City
    Reviewed by Theodore Strongin, "Mu-
        sic and Theater Share Same Circuit
        at Electric Circus," New York
        Times, July 10, 1968
    Commissioned by Jacob Glick

The Dying Alchemist
    Mixed media
    Manuscript in sketch

Valentine
    Four players with amplification
    Manuscript
    Premiered June 7, 1968, Carnegie
        Hall, New York City
    Commissioned by Gordon Mumma for
        Sonic Arts Group

1969   Aeolian Partitions
    Flute, clarinet, cello, and piano
    Published by Bowdoin College Press,
        1970
    Premiered May 17, 1969, Bowdoin
        College, Bowdoin, Maine
    Commissioned by Bowdoin College for
        Aeolian Players

A-OK
    Accordion, violins, chorus, conductor,
        audience, and tape-delay system
    Score published in Pavilion: Experi-
        ments in Art and Technology,
        edited by Billy Klüver, Julie Mar-
        tin, and Barbara Rose.   New York:
        Dutton, 1972, pp. 304-307
    Premiered February 23, 1969, Uni-
        versity of California, San Diego

Please Don't Shoot the Piano Player, He
Is Doing the Best He Can
    Mixed media
    Manuscript

Premiered October 1969, University
of California, Santa Barbara
Commissioned by Daniel Lentz for
California Time Machine

$s\gamma^*\gamma_d \mathcal{F}_{=1}$

Mixed media
Score published in <u>Source: Music of the</u>
<u>Avant Garde</u>, IV, 7, 52.
Premiered February 23, 1969, Uni-
versity of California, San Diego

The Dying Alchemist Preview
Trumpet, violin, percussion, narrator,
and slides by Lynn Lonidier
Manuscript
Premiered February 23, 1969, Uni-
versity of California, San Diego

The Wheel of Fortune
Clarinet, slides, monologue, and
costumes
Forthcoming from Smith Publications
Premiered October 14, 1970, Univer-
sity of Washington, Seattle
Reviewed by Wayne Johnson, "Oli-
veros Concert Is Fascinating Fun,"
Seattle Times, October 15, 1970
Composed for William O. Smith

1970   Link
Specialized and nonspecialized per-
formers
Published by Smith Publications as
Bonn Feier, 1977
Premiered May 5, 1972, Palomar
College, Oceanside, California
Commissioned by Larry Livingston
for Palomar College

Improvisations
_____

1963   Outline for Flute, Percussion, and String
Bass
Published by Media Press, 1971
Premiered May 10, 1963, Yale Uni-
versity, New Haven

Outline for Septet
   Accordion, trombone, trumpet, double
      bass, piano, and two percussionists
   Manuscript in sketch

1964   Fifteen for an Ensemble of Performers
   Instruments, singers, actors, and
      dancers
   Manuscript

1966   The C(s) for Once
   Trumpets, flutes, voices, organ, and
      three tape recorders
   Score is published in BMI Educational
      Journal Canavangard, 1971
   Premiered February 1966, Ann Arbor,
      Michigan

1967   Circuitry for Percussion and Light
   Manuscript
   Premiered June 1967, Mills College,
      Oakland

1968   "I Heard a Boy Singing ... "
   Manuscript

1970   Music for T'ai Chi
   Improvisation ensemble of accordion,
      two celli, and three voices
   Premiered August 22, 1970, Rancho
      Santa Fe, California

   To Valerie Solanas and Marilyn Monroe
   in Recognition of Their Desperation----
   Orchestra, chorus, organ, electronics,
      and lights
   Published by Smith Publications, 1977
   Chamber version premiered October 7,
      1970, Hope College, Holland, Mich-
      igan, and orchestra version pre-
      miered January 29, 1971, Grace
      Cathedral, San Francisco
   Reviewed by Donal Henahan, "Music:
      Work by Oliveros," New York
      Times, December 4, 1979; Tom
      Johnson, "American Composers'
      Orchestra," Village Voice, Decem-

ber 17, 1979; and Charles Shere,
"Pauline Oliveros Shows Feminism
Through Music," Oakland Tribune,
February 22, 1980

Why Don't You Write a Short Piece
Solo performer or group
Score published in Soundings, January
1972, p. 8
Premiered November 5, 1970, Uni-
versity of California, San Diego

1972   What to Do
Two or more performers
Published by Smith Publications, 1976

1975   Elephant Call
Solo trumpet
Manuscript
Premiered December 1975, San Diego
State University
Commissioned by Jack Logan

Rose Mountain Slow Runner
Voice and accordion
Manuscript
Broadcasted nationwide on National
Public Radio Stations, February
1976
Reviewed by Tom Johnson, "The Com-
poser Meditates," Village Voice,
October 10, 1977

1976   The Pathways of the Grandmothers
Accordion and voice
Manuscript
Premiered November 30, 1977, Art-
ists Coalition, San Diego

To Those in the Grey Northwestern
Rainforests
Unspecified ensemble
Score published in Zeitschrift,
Spring 1979, p. 81
Commissioned by Caldua Eclair

Willowbrook Generations and Reflections
Mixed winds, brasses, and voices

(twenty or more), or chorus alone
Published by Smith Publications, 1977
Premiered January 1976 by Willow-
    brook High School Band
Commissioned by Donald De Roche

1977   Horse Sings from Cloud
        Accordion and voice
        Manuscript
        Reviewed by John Rockwell, "New
            Music: Pauline Oliveros," New
            York Times, September 23, 1977

        King Kong Sing Along
        Chorus
        Manuscript
        Premiered June 1977, Annual Fest of
            the Avant Garde, World Trade
            Center, New York City

1978

        Bass drum with four players, four
            clarinets, eight tuned glasses, and
            solo chanter
        Published by Smith Publications, 1979
        Premiered April 1978, Independent
            Composers' Association, Los
            Angeles
        Reviewed by William Dunning, "At
            Both Ends of the Scale," Santa Fe
            Reporter, October 26, 1978
        Commissioned by Independent Com-
            posers' Association

1979   Double X
        Quartet or octet of instruments
        Manuscript
        Premiered August 17, 1979, Lenox
            Art Center, Lenox, Massachusetts
            (quartet version), and October 1979,
            San Francisco Conservatory (octet
            version)

        Rock Piece
        Any number of performers
        Manuscript
        Premiered August 17, 1979, Lenox
            Art Center, Lenox, Massachusetts

The Klickitat Ride
  Chorus and/or instruments and caller
  Manuscript
  Premiered April 8, 1979, Western
    Front, Vancouver, British Columbia

The Witness
  Virtuoso instrumentalists
  Forthcoming from Smith Publications
  Premiered May 30, 1980, The Kitchen,
    New York City
  Reviewed by Robert Palmer, "Avant-
    Garde: Miss Oliveros and Audi-
    ence," New York Times, June 2,
    1980
  Commissioned by Joseph Celli

1980 Anarchy Waltz
  Any number of performers
  Manuscript
  Premiered March 30, 1980, Cornish
    School, Seattle

Stacked Deck
  Music for play by Dick Higgins
  Manuscript
  Premiered January 10, 1982, Los
    Angeles County Museum of Art
  Written for Dick Higgins

Traveling Companions
  Percussion ensemble
  Forthcoming from Smith Publications
  Premiered May 1981, University of
    California, San Diego

1981 Monkey
  Children's ensemble
  Manuscript
  Premiered August 27, 1981, Cabrillo
    Music Festival, Aptos, California
  Reviewed by Josef Sekon, "A Most
    Enjoyable Event," Santa Cruz Sen-
    tinel, August 28, 1981; and Richard
    Pontzious, "Even the Participants
    Hated It," San Francisco Examiner,
    August 28, 1981

Lake CHARGOGGAGOGGMANCHAUGGA-
GOGGCHAUBUNABUNBAGAUGG
Any number of performers
Manuscript
Premiered November 1981, Cunning-
ham Foundation, New York City

Sonic meditations and ceremonial pieces

1970   Meditation on the Points of the Compass
Chorus, percussion, and audience
Published by Media Press, 1971
Premiered March 1970 during mid-
western tour of Illinois Wesleyan
Choir
Commissioned by David Nott

1971   Sonic Meditations I-XII
Specialized and nonspecialized musi-
cians
Published by Smith Publications, 1974
Reviewed by Tom Johnson, "Meditate
on Sound," Village Voice, May 24,
1976; and Nona Yarden, "A Medita-
tion," Perspectives of New Music,
XIX, 451-59
Dedicated to Amelia Earhart and the
♀ Ensemble

The Flaming Indian
Tape recorder and microphone
Published by Smith Publications, 1974
(available as variation of Sonic Med-
itation VIII)
Commissioned by Gerald Shapiro

1972   Sonic Images
Narrator and audience
Manuscript
Premiered September 23, 1972,
California State University, Los
Angeles

Phantom Fathom (II) from the Theater of
the Ancient Trumpeters: A Ceremonial Participation Evening
Any number of performers

Manuscript
Premiered July 19, 1972, California
State University, Long Beach

1973   Sonic Meditations XII-XXV
Specialized and nonspecialized musicians
Published by Smith Publications, 1974
Reviewed by Tom Johnson, "Meditate
on Sound," Village Voice, May 24,
1976

1974   A Ceremony of Sounds
Audience participation
Manuscript
Premiered April 1, 1975, University
of North Dakota, Grand Forks
Written for Tamar Reed

Crow Two--A Ceremonial Opera
Specialized and nonspecialized per-
formers
Score published in Desert Plants:
Conversations with 23 American
Musicians, by Walter Zimmermann.
Vancouver: Aesthetic Research
Centre of Canada, 1976, pp. a-k
(following p. 171), and forthcoming
from Smith Publications
Premiered March 6, 1975, University
of California, San Diego

1976   Cheap Commissions
Composer and individuals
Manuscript

1977   Rose Moon
Chorus and marathon runners
Published by Smith Publications, 1978
Premiered April 2, 1977, at Wesleyan
College, Middletown, Connecticut
Commissioned by Wesleyan College
for Wesleyan Singers

The Yellow River Map
Ceremonial meditation for a large
group
Score published in New Wilderness

Letter, December 1977/January
1978, pp. 22-23; and forthcoming
from Smith Publications
Premiered October 1977, Warwick,
New York
Commissioned by the Experimental
Intermedia Foundation, Elaine
Summers, director

1978   The Wheel of Life
            Vocal ensemble
            Manuscript

1979   Crow's Nest (The Tuning Meditation)
            Installation with film and dance
            Manuscript
            Premiered January 26, 1980, Guggen-
                heim Museum, New York City
            Reviewed by Charles Shere, "Weekend
                Provides Exciting Array of Con-
                certs in Eastbay," Oakland Tribune,
                February 18, 1980; and Tom John-
                son, "Aimless Major and Other
                Keys," Village Voice, March 31,
                1980

            El Relicario de los Animales
            Twenty instruments and singer
            Forthcoming from Smith Publications
            Premiered April 29, 1979, Contempo-
                rary Music Festival, California
                Institute of the Arts, Valencia
            Reviewed by Joan La Barbara, "New
                Music," High Fidelity/Musical
                America, August 1979, MA pp.
                8-9; and John Henken, "Contempo-
                rary Festival in Finale," Los An-
                geles Times, May 4, 1979

1980   Angels and Demons
            Any number of performers
            Manuscript
            Premiered March 30, 1980, Cornish
                School, Seattle
            Reviewed by Mark Swed, "Woman
                Composer Creates a World Apart,"
                Los Angeles Herald Examiner,

April 13, 1981; Colin Gardner,
"California Women Composers Concert," Los Angeles Times, April
14, 1981; and Richard Pontzious,
"Even the Participants Hated It,"
San Francisco Examiner, August
28, 1981

MMM, A Lullaby for Daisy Pauline
Audience participation
Manuscript
Premiered April 24, 1980, Walker
Art Center, Minneapolis
Reviewed by James E. Sellars, "Im-
provisations Enhance Concert,"
Hartford Courant, May 5, 1980

1981   Tashi Gomang
Orchestra
Forthcoming from Smith Publications
Premiered August 30, 1981, Cabrillo
Festival, Aptos, California
Reviewed by Bill Akers, "Festival
Ends on Memorable Note," (Cali-
fornia) Register-Pajaronian, August
31, 1981; Paul Hertelendy, "Oli-
veros Scales Cabrillo Heights,"
San Jose Mercury, September 1,
1981; and Rick Chatenever, "Ca-
brillo Music Festival's Triumphant
Conclusion," Santa Cruz Sentinel,
September 1, 1981

Miscellaneous compositions

1959   Horn Etudes
French horn
Manuscript

1969   California 99
Collaboration with Harold Budd, Larry
Austin, Daniel Lentz, Barney
Childs, Stanley Lunetta, John
Mizelle, David Sher, and Bertram
Turetzky
Manuscript

1972   Post Card Theater
       Solo performer
       Manuscript

1975   Theater of Substitution
       Solo performer
       Realizations published by Jackson
         MacLow, "being Pauline   narra-
         tive of a substitution," Big Deal,
         Fall 1976, pp. 168-176; and Pauline
         Oliveros, "Being Jackson," Paper
         Air Magazine, II, 3, 34
       Premiered August 1975, Camera Work
         Gallery, San Anselmo, California

       Unnatural Acts Between Consenting Adults
       Part of videotape series "Music with
         Roots in Aether" (1976), produced
         by Robert Ashley

1977   Theater of Substitution: Blind/Dumb/
       Director
       Solo performer
       Manuscript
       Premiered April 29-May 1, 1977,
         Center for Music Experiment, Uni-
         versity of California, San Diego

1980   Fwyynghn
       Theater collaboration with Gordon
         Mumma, Beatrice Manley, Linda
         Montano, and Louise Frasier
       Manuscript
       Premiered March 4, 1980, California
         Arts Festival, California Institute
         of the Arts, Valencia
       Reviewed by Martin Bernheimer,
         "Awful Opening for Cal-Arts Festi-
         val," Los Angeles Times, March 7,
         1980; and Melody Peterson, "Cal
         Arts' Contemporary Festival,"
         High Fidelity/Musical America,
         August 1980, MA pp. 30-31

PUBLISHERS' ADDRESSES

Aesthetic Research Center
P. O. Box 3044
Vancouver, BC V6B 3X5, Canada

Bowdoin College Press
Bowdoin College
Brunswick, ME   04011

Edition Tonos
Ahastrasse 7
Darmstadt, Germany

Media Press
Box 250
Elwyn, PA   19063

New Wilderness Letter
365 West End Avenue
New York, NY   10024

Smith Publications
2617 Gwynndale Avenue
Baltimore, MD   21207

DISCOGRAPHY

BYE BYE BUTTERFLY. New Music for Electronic and Recorded Media. Produced and edited by Charles Amirkhanian. 1750 Arch Records S-1765. Jacket notes by Charles Amirkhanian, 1977.

JAR PIECE. Electronic Essays. Marathon Music Incorporated MS2111 Canada.

I OF IV. New Sounds in Electronic Music. Produced by David Behrman. Odyssey 32 16 0160. Jacket notes contain information written by the composers.

OUTLINE FOR FLUTE, PERCUSSION, AND STRING BASS. The Contemporary Contrabass. Performances by Bertram Turetzky. Nonesuch H-71237. Jacket notes by Barney Childs, © 1971.

SOUND PATTERNS. Extended Voices: New Pieces for Chorus and for Voices Altered Electronically by Sound Synthesizers and Vocoder. Brandeis University Chamber Chorus directed by Alvin Lucier. Odyssey 32 16 0156. Jacket notes by Alvin Lucier.

SOUND PATTERNS. 20th Century Choral Music. University of Illinois New Music Choral Ensemble directed by Kenneth Gaburo. Ars Nova Ars Antigua Recordings.

TRIO FOR FLUTE, PIANO AND PAGE TURNER. New Music for Woodwinds. Advance Recordings FGR-9S.

BIBLIOGRAPHY

Material by Pauline Oliveros

"And Don't Call Them Lady Composers." New York Times, Septebmer 13, 1970.

"Being Jackson." Paper Air, II, 3, 34-35.

"Divisions Under Ground." Numus West, April 1973, pp. 35-40.

"Five Scenes." Numus West, Spring 1972, pp. 35-38.

Initiation Dream. Los Angeles: Astro Artz, 1982. [With Becky Cohen]

"Karl Kohn: Concerto Mutabile." Perspectives of New Music, Spring-Summer 1964, pp. 87-99.

"Many Strands." Numus West, March 1975, pp. 6-12.

"On Sonic Meditation." Painted Bride Quarterly, Winter 1976, pp. 54-69.

"On the Need for Research Facilities for New Music and Related Arts." Performing Arts Review, IX, 4 (1979), 464-472.

"Pauline Oliveros," in Klosty, James, editor, Merce Cunningham. New York: Dutton, 1975, pp. 79-80.

Pauline's Proverbs/Compiled by "Rosita"/Christmas 1976. Barrytown, N.Y.: Printed Editions, 1977.

"The Poetics of Environmental Sound." BMI Education Journal, Fall 1969.

[181]

"Single Stroke Roll Meditation (1973)."   Percussionist,
    Spring 1975, pp. 109-110.

"Software for People."   New Wilderness Letter, I, 7 (1979),
    40-46.

Software for People.   Barrytown, N.Y.:   Printed Editions,
    forthcoming.

"Some Sound Observations."   Source, II, 1 (January 1968),
    pp. 77-79.

"Sonic Meditations."   Source, V, 2 (1971), 103-107.

"Tape Delay Techniques for Electronic Music."   The Com-
    poser, I, 3 (December 1969), 135-142.

"Three Themes."   Numus West, January 1972, pp. 8-11.

"To Make a Universe of Sound: Four Visions."   Paid My
    Dues: Journal of Women and Music, II, 4 (Summer
    1978), 8-9.   [With Anna Rubin, Alison Howak, and
    Priscilla McLean.]

Manuscript material

La Jolla.   University of California at San Diego.   Pauline
    Oliveros' Archives.   "Career Narrative."

_____.   "Grant Proposal to Dr. Paul Saltman, Vice
    Chancellor/Academic Affairs, February 12, 1975."

_____.   "Memorandum for Meditation Project, January
    15, 1973.

_____.   "Theater Pieces."

Material about Pauline Oliveros

Anderson, Beth.   "Pauline Oliveros Was Here."   Soho
    Weekly News, February 20, 1980, pp. 43-45.

Baker's Biographical Dictionary. 6th ed. completely revised by Nicolas Slonimsky. New York: Schirmer, 1978.

Bennett, Myron. "Music as Furniture." High Fidelity/ Musical America, February 1972, pp. 65-66.

Cage, John. Notations. West Glover, Vt.: Something Else Press, 1969.

Childs, Barney. "Directions in American Composition Since the Second World War. Part II, 1960-1975." Music Educators Journal, March 1975, pp. 35-45.

Cope, David H. New Directions in Music. 2d ed. Dubuque, Iowa: Brown, 1976, pp. 37, 47, 59, 97, 108-109, 113, 157, 164, 201, 209-210, 211, 216, 220-221, and 250.

Dictionary of Contemporary Music. Edited by John Vinton. New York: Dutton, 1974.

Erickson, Robert. Sound Structure. Berkeley: University of California Press, 1975, p. 133.

Everett, Tom. "Five Questions, Forty Answers." The Composer, Fall 1971, p. 30.

Green Miriam. "Women: From Silence to Song." American Music Teacher, October 1974, p. 7.

Hamel, Peter. Through Music to the Self. Boulder, Colo.: Shambhala, 1979, pp. 184 and 202.

Hixon, Donald L. Women in Music: A Bibliography. Metuchen, N.J.: Scarecrow, 1975, p. 193.

Ingber, Lester. "Attention, Physics and Teaching." Journal for Social and Biological Studies, IV (1981), 225-235.

International Electronic Music Catalog. Compiled by Hugh Davies. Cambridge: M.I.T. Press, 1968, pp. 21, 175, 178-179, 209, 291.

Karkoschka, Erhard. Notation in New Music. New York: Praeger, 1972, pp. 122, 132, and 156-161.

Kefalas, Elinor. "Pauline Oliveros: An Interview."

[184] The Music of Pauline Oliveros

High Fidelity/Musical America, June 1975, pp. MA 24-25.

Klüver, Billy, Julie Martin, and Barbara Rose, editors. Pavilion. New York: Dutton, 1972, pp. 304-307.

La Barbara, Joan. "New Music." High Fidelity/Musical America, September 1977, pp. MA 11-12.

Le Page, Jane Weiner. Women Composers and Conductors. Metuchen, N.J.: Scarecrow, 1980, pp. 165-190.

MacLow, Jackson. "being Pauline   narrative of a substitution." Big Deal, Fall 1976, pp. 168-176.

Montano, Linda. Art in Everyday Life. Barrytown, N.Y.: Printed Editions, 1981.

New Grove Dictionary of Music and Musicians. London: Macmillan, 1980.

Osterreich, Norbert. "Music with Roots in the Aether." Perspectives of New Music, XVI (1977), 216 and 222-223.

Percival, John. Experimental Dance. New York: Universe, 1971, pp. 46-47.

Pool, Jeannie G. "America's Women Composers: Up from the Footnotes." Music Educators Journal, January 1979, pp. 35-36.

Rockwell, John. "The Musical Meditations of Pauline Oliveros." New York Times, May 25, 1980.

Roth, Moria. "An Interview with Pauline Oliveros." New Performance, I, 2 (1977), 41-51.

Schnorbus, Joan. "The Unexpected Music." San Dieguito Citizen, June 7, 1978.

Schwartz, Elliott. "Directions in American Composition Since the Second World War. Part I, 1945-1960." Music Educators Journal, February 1975, p. 38.

_____. Electronic Music: A Listener's Guide. New York: Praeger, 1973, pp. 84-85, 112, 122, 124, 193-195, and 246-249.

Skowronski, Jo Ann. Women in American Music: A Bibliography. Metuchen, N.J.: Scarecrow, 1978.

Spizizen, Louise. "Composers of Area Code 714--Part II, Composers of Academe." Applause Magazine, October 1978, p. 24.

Springer, P. Gregory. "The Nonpareils of Pauline Oliveros." The Advocate, February 22, 1979.

Strange, Allen. Electronic Music. Dubuque, Iowa: Brown, 1972, pp. 8, 93, 95, and 137.

Subotnick, Morton. "Pauline Oliveros, Trio." Perspectives of New Music, Fall-Winter 1963, pp. 77-82.

Von Gunden, Heidi. "The Theory of Sonic Awareness in The Greeting by Pauline Oliveros." Perspectives of New Music, Spring-Summer, 1981, pp. 409-416.

Who's Who in America. 42nd ed. Chicago: Marquis Who's Who, 1982.

Yarden, Nona. "A Meditation." Perspectives of New Music, XIX (1980-81), 451-459.

Zimmermann, Walter, ed. Desert Plants: Conversations with 23 American Musicians. Vancouver: Aesthetic Research Center, 1976, pp. 163-182.

INDEX